MONIQUE CARLYLE

An illustrated practical guide for new dog owners
with room to document and track your progress.

Puppy

Handbook

Your Dog's First Year

Hardcover ISBN: 978-1-7392150-1-9
Paperback ISBN: 978-1-7392150-0-2
E-Book ISBN: 978-1-7392150-2-6

Puppy Handbook

Written by Monique Carrie
Cover Art by Monique Carrie
Layout by Monique Carrie
Edited by Pam Elise Harris

www.bymoniquecarrie.com

Disclaimer

The author is not a veterinary specialist, dog behaviourist or nutritionist. This book and the content provided herein is simply for educational purposes and do not take the place of any professional advice. We have made every effort to ensure that the content provided in this book is accurate and helpful for our readers at publishing time. However, this is not an exhaustive treatment for your dog. Although the author has made every effort to ensure that the information in this book is correct at press time, the author does not assume and disclaim any liability to any party for any loss, damage, or disruption caused by errors or omissions, whether such errors or omissions result from negligence, accident, or any other cause. You are responsible for your own choices, actions and results. You should consult a specialist for your specific dog's problems, questions and needs.

THIS
Handbook
Belongs To

Owner Name
_____

Dog Name
_____

*To all dog owners who never stop learning
and do not fear admitting that they love their
pups like their own children.*

CONTENT

ABOUT
THE **Author**

Growing up with dogs meant I learned from a young age how to take care of them, especially as often I had to do most of the walks and training. I've learned a lot of tips and tricks along the way and wanted to share them and make every dog parent's life easier.

Recently, I finally got the chance to get my first dog as a grown-up, and I have more responsibility, as now I have to take care him of mostly on my own. I've gathered all my knowledge in one place and have been saving information about the best food, toys and games for many years. I wanted to create something that would help both new puppy parents and people who have been pup parents for a long time.

What you will find in this handbook?

This comprehensive *Puppy Handbook* is perfect for pup parents who want to help their dog grow into a well-behaved and healthy adult. With guides on training, health and food, you can keep track of what works and what doesn't with your pup, making this handbook a cherished keepsake.

Well-behaved dogs rely on routines, and this guidebook is based on the premise that if you accustom your dog to a certain routine from puppyhood, he or she will be more relaxed and less likely to get into trouble.

With age comes wisdom!

Or so it goes . . . Let us not forget that we all stay childish in one way or another, so don't be too hard on your dog.

Connect with me:

@monique_carrie   www.bymoniquecarrie.com

Georgie
My precious little baby

HOW TO USE
THIS **Book**

Tips for busy dog parents

Keep it near

Put it somewhere where it is easy to look at and refer back to. We do not want an "out of sight, out of mind" situation where you bought this handbook and left it somewhere and forgot about it.

Because if you can get to it easily and reference it, you will help yourself and your pup.

Designate time

Choose one time during the day, for example after breakfast or before bed, when you are free to dedicate ten to fifteen minutes of your day to go through the pages.

Find time every day to train your dog. Even if it's ten minutes, your future self will thank you.

Be consistent

Sticking to a schedule, having quality time and following up with regular sessions will help you keep your puppy on track and achieve the best results.

That goes for everyone in the household. Dogs get confused and anxious with inconsistency and mixed messages.

Write it down

If you find you are still struggling with your responsibilities, this handbook can be a source of support.

If your pup gifts you with a funny story, write it down, and you can always refer to later or share with your friends and family.

Share the responsibility

This is not only a handy puppy manual but also a perfect training tool for your kids or other family members.

Be patient

This is a tool. It will not morph your dog overnight. There is no magic trick that will make your dog obedient. Give yourself and your pup time to learn and grow.

It takes around one hundred repetitions of a command before it's mastered by your pup, of course, depending on the dog and the breed.

Introduction

Creating this book for me was simply out of a genuine passion for dogs. I love spending time with my pup Georgie, a big-hearted, friendly, sweet Labrador. We fill our days with runs in the woods, playing with toys, training and mastering established and new commands, and of course – lots of belly rubs. Then, when he goes into one of his long naps, I can finally focus on my work.

I believe that with my experience of raising my dogs, I will guide you through this exciting new journey you are undertaking. By the time you have finished this handbook, you will understand how to create as good a bond with your new pup, as I have with Georgie. Most importantly, you will understand how to guide your dog to make the right decisions.

The bond with dogs is special, in the way dog and owner communicate with each other from their hearts. Dogs are a part of our lives, and it shows in our history, culture and art. I want to help your pup to grow to be a happy, healthy and well-behaved dog.

I hope that before you have got a dog, you have done your research. By this point, you know that as a puppy owner you will have a full-time job and commitment for ten to fifteen years. Dogs require time, space, attention and sometimes a sizeable chunk of your budget. All in all for me, personally, it took six months to prepare for Georgie to come into our lives.

If a dog is for you, after doing all your research and evaluation, it may be time to welcome a puppy into your life, a new family member to grow and strengthen your bond with and to learn, love and form a friendship that will last a lifetime.

You will find detailed instructions on how to take care of and raise your puppy. For all dog owners, a well-behaved, happy, healthy dog is a pleasure. This handbook is here to help you through the first twelve months with your puppy. Those months are the most crucial and important ones. Remember to keep the handbook near, as you don't have to remember all the information at once. You just need to have it handy for every question.

LET'S GET
STARTED

CHAPTER
ONE

YOUR DOG'S Profile

Space for
your puppy
picture

Name _____

Number of sibilings _____

Birth date _____

Space for a
picture
with the littler

Mummy picture

Daddy picture

MOTHER

Name _____

Breed _____

Health _____

Kennel Club Number

_____

FATHER

Name _____

Breed _____

Health _____

Kennel Club Number

_____

CHARACTER

_____
_____
_____
_____
_____
_____
_____
_____
_____
_____
_____

CHARACTER

_____
_____
_____
_____
_____
_____
_____
_____
_____
_____
_____

Puppy

DETAILS:

Gender

Breed

ADOPTION:

Shelter/Breeder _____

Name _____

Phone _____

Adoption Day _____

PERSONALITY:

AFFECTIONATE

CHILD FRIENDLY

CONFIDENCE

EASY TO TRAIN

ENERGY LEVEL

FOOD MOTIVATION

FRIENDLINESS

INTELLIGENCE

NEEDY

PET FRIENDLY

PLAYFULNESS

STUBBORN

TRAINABILITY

Profile

CHARACTERISTIC:

Coat colour _____

Eye colour _____

Unique markings _____

Allergies _____

BREED CHARACTERISTICS:

Breed originated in

_____

Bred to

_____

Good at

_____

Bad at

_____

Prone to

_____

Weight

_____   Height

_____   _____

Body specifications

_____

Life span

_____

YOUR DOG Details

MICROCHIP NUMBER

Number:

Type :

KENNEL REGISTRATION NUMBER

Kennel name :

Unique ownership number:

Registration or stud book number:

Owner name :

Collection date :

VETERINARY CLINIC

Name :

Address :

Phone number :

Email:

THE OWNER Details

Name :	
Gender:	
Address :	
Mobile:	

Owner picture

DOG
SITTER & Kennel

DAY CARE & KENNEL

Name :	
Number :	
Address :	
Rates :	
Other services :	

SITTER

Name :	
Number :	
Location :	
Email address :	
Rates :	

SITTER RESPONSIBILITIES

Dog:	
Clean:	
Plants:	
Take out the trash :	

THE DOG Insurance

THE COMPANY

Name :

Website:

Mobile:

Email :

Log in email:

Log in password:

YOUR PLAN

Annual coverage :

Claim contribution:

Payment plan :

SUBLIMITS

Complimentary treatment:

Behaviour treatment :

Dental treatment :

Theft or stray :

23

CHAPTER
TWO

PREPARING
FOR YOUR
Puppy

SHOULD YOU GET A Puppy?

Getting a dog is an enormous responsibility, but when you are deciding if you should get one, weigh both pros and cons. As much as it is fun playing and cuddling with your puppy, it is a commitment to look after your new furry friend for ten to fifteen years.

PROS	CONS
Dogs offer unconditional love. Your pup will bring love and joy to your life on an ongoing basis. It will love you regardless of whether you are having a bad or good day.	Puppies require a lot of time and attention, especially in the first couple of years. When you want to go away, you have to always make a plan of who will look after your dog.
Your pup will keep you company. There is no honour that compares to a dog with their loyalty. Dogs make you feel safe and secure.	Besides the initial cost you pay, there will be monthly costs for your dog such as food, treatments. vet visits, day care, insurance and toys.
Improving your lifestyle and wellbeing. Besides the daily exercise you will gain together, also it has been proved that dogs help fight depression and anxiety.	Finding time every day – morning and evening, sunny or rainy – to walk your dog and not just to take it out to have a toilet break. Well-behaved dogs are tired dogs.
Learning to interact with a dog will help you grow your personality and gain skills you will use throughout your life. Such as looking after another being, planning, training, being assertive and more.	You will find dog hair everywhere, parts of a chewed toys and more. Your cleaning efforts will probably double up, especially at the beginning, whilst your doggy is still being potty trained.

HOW MUCH DOES
IT COST TO OWN A Dog?

The lifetime cost of a dog will widely vary depending on the breed of your dog, the size of your dog, lifespan, health, and if your dog is bought or adopted. Below, you can see a breakdown of each type of cost. To give you an estimate figure, for a medium-sized healthy dog living up to twelve years old, their lifetime cost can be around £31,020.

Lifetime Estimate	Breakdown
Initial cost = £1500 to £4000	If you are adopting a dog from a shelter, you might spend no more than £500, but if you are buying from a breeder, you might spend up to £3500. Adding to that are all the items you need to begin with that can be around £600.
Health costs = £6420 (Lifetime)	Yearly cost for flea and worming treatments around £150; neutering up to £350; booster vaccinations £35; ad hoc health needs £200. Note that older dogs can require pricy surgeries or treatments.
Food = £14,400 (Lifetime)	Monthly food cost will depend on the size of your dog. For a medium-sized dog, the cost is £70 to £150 per month depends on the type and brand. Puppy food is more expensive, but as they get older, their calories intake gets lower.
Accessories = £7,200 (Lifetime)	Harness, leads, leash, toys, bowls, beds, fleeces, towers and more can get pricy. Your puppy will chew them off quickly or some will just get damaged over time. Yearly, you will spend around £500 to £800 in total.

WHAT IS THE DIFFERENCE

BETWEEN GETTING A DOG FROM A BREEDER AND ADOPTING A

Rescue Dog?

Getting a purebred pup or a rescue is one of the most common debates in the pet industry, and I know it to make the right decision for you.

People will always have an opinion about whether you should adopt or buy a dog. Some people will tell you that you should not support the breeding industry and to adopt a homeless dog, and others will tell you that rescue dogs are hard work and just get a puppy.

I will not be telling you whether you should or should not get a rescue or buy from a breeder. I will simply explain to you the differences in having one as a pet.

Some rescue dogs come with special needs

Most likely, the shelter will tell you in advance about the special needs of the dog, but you really need to factor this into your time and effort. Does the dog have a disability, is the dog with a traumatic past and has trust issues, or is the dog just getting older? You will need to be patient and understanding. Of course, you will have to approach the training differently, have experience with dogs, and knowledge of their body language. It is essential when owning a rescue dog with special needs.

For some people, getting a dog from a breeder is the best option because they know what traits the dog will have if they are raising it to be a working dog or if they have young children around.

Often with a rescue dog, if you don't know its history, you are taking a higher risk as you don't know what traits it might develop, how big it's going to get, and how it will react to situations you put it in. Plus, if you have children under five, the shelter might not even allow you to adopt the dog, as it has not been socialised around children.

On the other hand, you are getting a grown dog, which will be calmer, and you will know all its quirks before getting it.

In most cases you will adopt a grown dog

This means the dog has already formed its views and understandings about the world, and it will already have habits and behaviours. Sometimes, you might get a well-behaved and trained dog. Other times, you might need to spend extra time reforming and retraining old habits.

Little to no information about the dog

This means you won't know if they have inherited diseases, if they have trained much, if they are aggressive, or if they need a lot of attention. With a specific breed from a licenced breeder, you will have a full health history of the parents and specific traits in your dog.

BREEDER'S
RED Flags

The purchase of a new pup is an exciting time for many people. After all, you're taking home your own lifelong companion. So how can you be sure your potential new family member has been looked after properly? What should you look for when vetting a dog breeder and what are some red flags that should make you think twice? Let's inspect what you should pay attention to when shopping for a dog breeder.

1 Lack of transparency

The most obvious red flag, but it's also a dead giveaway. If someone gets funny about your questions or doesn't want to show you where their dogs are being kept, then no matter what excuses they come up with, just walk away from that situation and find somewhere else.

2 They are giving the pups before they are eight weeks

It means that they have separated these animals from their mother too early, which can lead to health problems down the road. The pups will be malnourished and will not have the chance to learn important lessons about eating, drinking, toilet and socialisation.

3 Pushy sell

If a breeder is playing on your fear of missing out and asking for a non-refundable deposit without you even meeting the dogs – run. Refusing any kind of money protection scheme makes you an easy target for a scam. Walk away if someone says no when asked about refundable deposits and pushes you. These aren't businesses worth dealing with.

4 Offering multiple breeds

Breeders who offer more than one breed are often dog mills, not responsible and caring people. True breed lovers will have a love for their particular type of animal and will look after it thoroughly. They won't just be in it to make money off farming dogs.

5 You can't meet any of the dogs' parents

While visiting the breeder, seeing all parties involved will give the most realistic sense. The breeder most likely has paid for a stud, so you can't see the dad and his role in raising these pups together, but you should meet the mum. You need to see her and the pups during feedings or playtime to get a feeling of how those who raised him interact and the character of your chosen pup.

6 A large number of puppies available

The number of puppies that a breeder can have at any time is dependent on the quality and age range for both dad, as well as mum. Responsible breeders should follow best practice, which suggests 4-6 litters per dog with an average litter size between 6 - 8 pups per birth; and not over one or two litters per year. If a breeder has puppies available all the time, it's a concerning factor for the health of the mum and the pup and if the breeder is running actually a puppy farm.

7 Lack of health records

Do the parent dogs have their hips, elbows and hearts certified through OFA (Orthopaedic Foundation for Animals) or PennHIP? A reputable breeder will be proud to show you the results of any or all testing done on their dogs as well as provide copies of any testing done on their parents. You should have proof that they tested both mum and dad for their breed predisposition diseases. The breeder should show you the health history of these parents. They can pass serious health problems to your pup from these breeding grounds and can lead to a lifetime of suffering or even premature death.

8 Lack of documentation

Documentation is the key to everything when you're dealing with a breeder. They should have documentation on file from their association. For the parents, they should have health records, the kennel club registration, family tree and their microchip number. For your future pup, you should have KLC registration, microchip number, health check, vaccinations, worming and flea treatment and a puppy contract.

If you see any of these signs, you are dealing with an unethical or unlicensed breeder that you should not do business with. Continue searching or adopt from either a shelter or rescue organisation. There a plenty of dogs waiting for your love.

HOW MUCH OF A TIME
COMMITMENT IS A Pup?

Dogs are pack animals and do not thrive on being left alone for long periods of time. They want to be included and be part of the family. So when you bring a dog into your life, prepare for the responsibilities that come with that.

On average, per day, you will spend around two hours and fifteen minutes' active time with your pup. Of course, it could be more or less if your dog is big or small. Bigger dogs require around one hour and thirty minutes of daily exercise, with smaller dogs, thirty minutes can be enough.

Besides the active time you have to spend with your furry friend, it will need to have company for about eight hours in total. Different breeds and unique character will tolerate a different amount of time being left alone, but most of the time five hours is the optimal.

As your dog ages, it will be content with less play and more naps, so your active time spend with them will be less when they are younger.

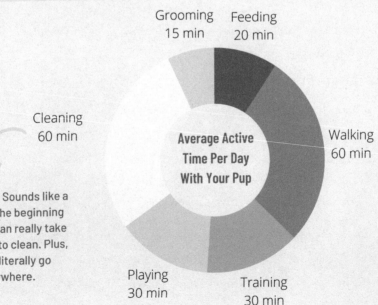

Grooming
15 min

Feeding
20 min

Cleaning
60 min

Yes, I know. Sounds like a lot, but at the beginning accidents can really take a long time to clean. Plus, hair will literally go everywhere.

Average Active Time Per Day With Your Pup

Walking
60 min

Playing
30 min

Training
30 min

DO YOU NEED A PET
Insurance?

One thing that many new dog owners are unsure about is pet insurance. Pet insurance can help you pay for veterinary costs if your dog gets sick or injured but won't cover routine and or preventative exams. Most vets will recommend pet insurance, as it can help avoid putting your pet down, due to lack of funds to cover the medical care.

The cost of pet insurance varies depending on the plan, the age and breed of your dog, but it is less expensive than paying for pricy veterinary emergencies out of pocket. Monthly plans start from £10 and can go up to £100 for the most premium ones. I advise you to do thorough research. The younger and healthier the dog is, the better plan you will get.
With that in mind, it is an individual decision. To help you make the best possible decision, I've listed everything you need to take into consideration.

Benefits		Negatives
It protects you from potential financial liability if your pet gets injured or becomes ill with a long-term health condition.		Most insurances have a claim contribution minimum. If your bill is under it, the insurance won't cover it. Also, some insurances refuse pre-existing, long lasting or breed specific conditions.
It helps you keep peace of mind with this investment that in an event that your fur baby gets lost, gets stolen or passes away, you will be reimbursed.		You might never need this type of coverage, and you are paying ultimately for "what ifs".
Pet insurance covers long term dental care for conditions that could be expensive to treat.		Pet insurance is a reimbursement scheme, so ultimately you handle all veterinary cost, until your claim is accepted, even then it won't cover the full cost.

To make a final decision, do a cost analysis to see how much you will pay on insurance and then compare it with the amount you are spending now for vet bills. After evaluating the costs, decide which option will be best for you.

You should take into consideration your pet's health and its parents, as the best time to get an insurance is when they are young and don't have conditions; therefore, you can get the best.

BEFORE GETTING
YOUR PUPPY Checklist

Shopping list:

- Adjustable collar
- Harness
- Comfortable leash
- ID tag
- Food and water bowl
- Food and training treats
- Treat pouch
- Poop bags
- Poop bag holder
- Crate and crate cover
- Bed
- Potty pads
- Nail clippers
- Hair brush and clippers
- Water bottle
- Toys - chew, chase, and puzzle
- Pooper scooper
- Grooming wipes
- Ear cleaner
- Dog toothpaste
- Dog toothbrush
- Dog shampoo and conditioner
- Dog washing brush
- Paw cleaner
- Antiseptic spray for cuts
- Enzyme spray for accidents
- Carpet cleaner
- Pet hair dissolver for washing machines
- Clothes hair remover
- Towels and blankets

Before choosing the puppy ask:

- Is the breeder licensed?
- Have you seen the mother?
- Have you seen the father?
- Have you seen a family tree of the parents?
- Do you have the parents Kennel Club Numbers?
- Have the parents been screened for health conditions?
- How many litters has the mother had?
- How old is the mother?
- Have you visited the puppy at their birth home?
- Have you read the puppy contract?
- Has it been wormed?
- Has it been flea treated?
- Has it had its immunisations?
- Are the puppies Kennel Club registered?
- Will the puppies be micro-chipped?
- Are the puppies being socialised?
- Is the deposit secured?
- When was it born?
- How old will it be when it's able to leave?
- What is the history of the puppy, if it's from a shelter?
- When has it been weaned from the mum?
- Has it been potty trained?
- What food has it been given?
- Has it been crate trained?

What to bring with you on the day you are taking you puppy home?

- Puppy travelling crate
- Collar
- Leash
- Treats and treats pouch
- Chewy toy
- Blanket with the mother's scent
- Water bottle

AFTER GETTING
YOUR PUPPY Checklist

Preparing your home

- Separate a puppy area
- Remove hazardous materials
- Secure your yard
- Set a schedule

Essential Services:

- Veterinarian
- Insurance
- Pet Sitter
- Dog Walker
- Dog Groomer
- Dog Trainer
- Obedience Classes
- Doggy Day Care/Kennel

Once you get your puppy you need to:

- Have the documents for the microchip
- Have the documents of the Kennel Club registration
- Have the family tree if its Kennel Club registered
- Take it to the vet within a week of getting it
- Have changed the ownership name to yours
- Have a confirmation of your payment
- Have the signed puppy contract with you
- Know what vaccination it has had
- Know when is it next vaccination due
- Know when is it next flea treatment due and what type
- Know when is it the next worming treatment due and what type

Training

- Socialise
- Desensitise
- Learn dogs' body language
- Positive reinforcement

Notes

_____
_____
_____
_____
_____
_____
_____
_____
_____
_____
_____
_____
_____
_____
_____
_____
_____
_____
_____
_____

ROADMAP TO
A SUCCESSFUL Transition

Congratulations on your new family addition. To ensure you have smooth first weeks, start with training from the first day.

1 Make sure the house rules are taught from the beginning.

It's important to remember your puppy doesn't understand the expectations of its owners. As Dr Ian Dunbar, veterinarian, animal behaviourist, and dog trainer said, "If you want your dog to follow the rules of the house, by all means, do not keep them a secret."

2 Give your puppy time to adjust to its new life and home.

As excited as you are to show it to friends and family, keep in mind that this period is very stressful for your puppy. Socialising should be done gradually.

3 Keep your dog away from trouble.

You need to supervise your dog if you want it to stay safe and your home to remain protected. When this is not possible, keep your dog in a safe place like a "doggy den."

4 Your dog's home area should be restricted.

Immediately allowing your new dog free access to the entire house can cause disaster. They may develop any number of bad habits. First, make sure they have the right habits before you give them freedoms.

Remember, good habits are just as hard to remember as bad ones. It will take time and patience to master each positive command.

5   Show your dog his designated toilet area.

You should take your dog to that area every hour. If they do not relieve themselves, put them in their doggy den. Praise and reward them for each successful potty break. Ignore the mistakes or unsuccessful attempts.

6   Don't punish your dog. Redirect it.

Dogs won't understand why you are mad at them, so correct, never punish them, and redirect them by showing them what you would like them to do instead.

7   Create a puppy schedule

It will amaze you how quickly your furry pal will settle into the daily routine of its life! Feeding times, potty breaks, playtimes, exercise sessions and training sessions are all included. See page 203.

8   Start with obedience training right away.

Determine who in your household will be responsible for training your dog. During the first few weeks, the feeding time should be used as training time. In case you do not have time, enrol your puppy at a puppy school or meet a certified dog trainer. Be calm and consistent whenever you are training your pet.
More on chapter nine, page 190.

WITH **First Day**
YOUR PUPPY

Now that you've brought home your puppy, it may be hard to remember what life was like before. You'll need to be aware of some new things and then meet the challenges of getting a puppy acclimated to its new home. It won't take long before you both settle into a routine and this will just be another day. But until then, here are some tips on transitioning as seamlessly as possible.

Put the blanket and or toy that you took from the breeder or shelter into their crate. The familiar smell of home will make them more willing to come into their crate, and it will help build their trust in your ability to keep them safe.

It's normal for your new friend to be nervous at first. To help with their first day experience, minimise loud noises, don't have too many people in the room at once, and do not have bright lights and scary sounds.

Allow it to get familiar with its puppy area – sniff and investigate. Let it get comfortable, and then you can train it.

Some dogs will take a bit of coaxing to come when called, so it's good to carry a small treat with you at first, just in case they are more interested in the flooring than you.

It's very important to establish your dog's routine on their first day. They need to know when, where, and how they get their food, water, and bathroom breaks.

HOW TO
Pup Proof
YOUR HOME

Puppies are curious by nature. Because everything smells like their surroundings, they're always sniffing around. They will explore every crack and crevice to find out what might be in there. Exploring means sniffing, digging and chewing – all-natural behaviours for dogs and especially puppies. To avoid creating hazardous situations and bad habits, it is best to pup proof your home before you bring your new pet.

1 Clear the Space

Take out or put away anything that your dog might chew on, eat, or destroy that you care about – clothes, shoes, make-up, children's toys, books, phones, blankets, cushions, trash, etc.

2 Hide Toys

Do not place your dog's toys in areas your dog can reach, as not all of them are chewer-proof. As your puppy is growing its new teeth, anything that might be chewed and swallowed should be put away. Separate them. More on page 42.

3 Create a Puppy Den

Create a "pet area" with gates and such, where your puppy is free to play and explore even when you are not supervising it. Ideally should be near their bed, so it's their own little area of the house so that they don't get into trouble and know they go to sleep in their crate when they want to.

4 Keep Food and Products Away

Keep all yours and your dog's food treats and medications locked in a cabinet that has a child lock. And leave no food or cleaning products where your dog can reach them. Don't leave knives, plates, toxic plants, glasses or cups on the kitchen counter unattended – even if it's just for a few seconds. It is all it takes for a fatal accident to happen.

5 Hide Cables

Keep all your computer, TV, stereo and other cables put away and out of reach. Dogs are attracted by the smell of wires and anything that's plugged in. Keep all electrical cords off the floor.

CREATING THE
Puppy Area

The Den

Your puppy needs a place that's just its. For it, the best of all worlds would be an area with plenty of space to play and explore, safely and away from trouble, as well as somewhere warm and soft on which they can feel safe at night when sleeping or resting during day-to bedtime routines!

Position this cosy nest close enough so you're able to keep tabs but far away from busy proceedings back home. Let your furry friend have peace in his own personal oasis before tiring him out too much with activity.

Under observation, you could also bring your other pets into the den to get to know their new friend and play with each other, but do not leave them alone at the beginning.

Crates are proven to minimise the destruction of your home and make life easier for both pup AND owners. Crates help dogs to feel more secure, and you'll be able to supervise them while they sleep.

The first two weeks of a puppy's life are an extremely critical time for developing great habits like not chewing on shoes or scratching on furniture. If they already spent time confined at the breeder or shelter, then this will be familiar ground, which makes things go more smoothly during the introductory period.

Your pup needs to feel comfortable in its crate, but you don't want it spending more than about three hours at a time there at the beginning. Of course, it can sleep overnight with no problem as long as it gets some toilet breaks and you always allow it out when necessary. As it grows, and its bladder gets bigger and they learn to hold it, your pup won't need to get in the middle of the night to have a wee.

The crate is a space only for your new puppy, and it should not share it with other pets, and you or your children should not be getting in the crate with the dog, even if it's a game.

Before leaving your pup unsupervised, always remove your puppy's collar, leads and clothes because they are all choking hazards.

On page 149, we will look into how to crate train your dog and yourself, as the first week is the hardest.

Position the crate in a place where there is little noise, activity, direct sunlight and draught. Otherwise, the pup might become too wrapped up in its feelings of safety! Ideally, the crate should be set up in the corner of a room.

I would recommend getting a cover for the crate, so it protects it from noise and other distractions when it's inside. Put potty training pads, blankets (no beds with padding, as it will get chewed and destroyed) and only chew-proof toys and maybe treat the dispenser inside the crate. In short, make the crate comfortable and safe.

It's important to keep the crate cosy and clean, as dogs dislike sleeping in dirt.

THE IMPORTANCE OF

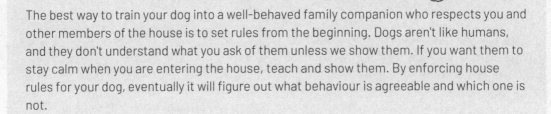

House Rules

The best way to train your dog into a well-behaved family companion who respects you and other members of the house is to set rules from the beginning. Dogs aren't like humans, and they don't understand what you ask of them unless we show them. If you want them to stay calm when you are entering the house, teach and show them. By enforcing house rules for your dog, eventually it will figure out what behaviour is agreeable and which one is not.

Many people think that establishing house rules for the dog will restrict its freedom, but this isn't true.

General advice from most dog trainers is to have stricter rules for the first two years until your dog is more mature and less impulsive.

Rules, which are consistent and fair, will teach your dog how to behave in a situation. Once your dog has earned your trust, you can start having exceptions, but it must win its freedom.

You wouldn't allow a toddler or a teenager to do as it pleases, right? In that case, why should you allow your young dog?

The rules are not only for your dog but for you and the rest of the household.

Remember to:

1. Set the rules from day one.
2. Be consistent with the rules.
3. Be consistent with the consequences.
4. Be calm when you redirect your dog if they made a mistake.
6. Don't punish your dog.
7. Your pooch must earn its freedom. We should not give it away.

Here are a few examples of rules for dogs that you will benefit from having in your house:

ADOPTED

On page 207, you can write down your own house rules.

1. Your dog is to wait for a release command before it can eat.

2. Your dog is to leave everything that has fallen on the floor.

3. Your dog is to sit in its place when any family member is having a meal.

4. Your dog must not jump on any person or pet in the house.

5. Your dog is to be potty trained.

6. Your dog is not to be allowed on any furniture.

7. Your dog is allowed only in certain areas of the house.

8. Your dog can't roam around freely in the house or yard.

9. Your dog may not chew anything other than allocated toys.

10. Your dog must wait by doors and gates for the release command.

WHY YOU SHOULD
CATEGORISE YOUR DOG'S
TOYS

If your dog has lots of toys, you might think it's okay to just let them all mingle in the room with no thought about where they're going. But soon you will notice two things. First, your dog will start getting bored with the toys, and second, it will stop associating play and fun time with you. What happens when your dog thinks you're boring? It will stop listening to you when there is anything your pup finds exciting – a fresh smell, a dog, a squirrel to chase, and the list goes on. The bottom line is that you will be less able to train your dog into obedience.

Why let that happen? Why not give your dog the best of everything? Why not get a toy box and sort all your canine's toys into a few categories, so you can choose the perfect toy for each situation from day-to-day?

Categories

Interactive toys

These are so-called puzzle toys, where your dog needs to work for their food or treat. You should give your dog these toys only under supervision. They are a great mental exercise for your dog, as they have to work their brain and use their senses to solve the puzzle. Such toys are perfect for all dogs prone to destructive behaviour due to boredom.

Often used in enrichment activities. More on page 196.

Boredom toys

These are the safest and most common toys you feel comfortable giving your dog have free access to. Essentially, most of your dog's toys. To help with keeping the toys interesting, hide some away, from time to time, and re-introduce them. Ropes, rubber rings, ragged toys, etc.

Chewy

In some cases, we need to leave our dogs with something to keep them occupied because we are leaving for a prolonged period or just so that they have a mental outlet while we are busy. In these cases, these toys come in handy. They are made from hard-to-chew materials – high-grade rubber toys, antlers, nylabones, etc. The dog will enjoy chewing them, doing no damage to their gums or teeth. Also, these toys often help in keeping dental hygiene in good shape.

Playtime toys

These are toys whose main purpose is to be played with another human and your pooch. We can use them in games like tugging or fetch, but it is important that we use the toys for such purpose only, and the human starts and ends the game before the dog gets bored.

Outdoors toys

These should be your dog's favourite toys, that your dog associates with having the best time with you – outside. Remember to keep these toys only for play on your walks. They can be balls, flirt poles, frisbees, ropes or anything your dog loves. It's important to have these toys of a high value in your dog's eyes, as you can use them to get its attention when it gets distracted by the environment.

CHAPTER THREE

D O G
BREED
Groups

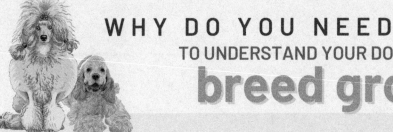

WHY DO YOU NEED
TO UNDERSTAND YOUR DOG
breed group?

For generations, humans have been breeding dogs in order to create new breeds to suit their needs as owners and perform practical tasks for them. Most dogs served the humans who owned them, but over time and continuing diversification, some dogs were bred purely for companionship.

How does breeding work?

It's when you select two dogs for their genetic traits (physical or characteristically) and then breed them, hoping their offspring will have the same traits. Breeding dogs is not just about aesthetics but also about behaviour.

In 2009, the American Kennel Club redefined dog breeds into seven groups to combine and define and group all breeds. To understand your dog's needs better, you need to understand its breed; you need to know which group it belongs and what was is the purpose of the breed.

Herding	Sporting
Hound	Working
Terrier	Non-Sporting

Toy

Once you understand the breed group your dog comes from, you will have to dive into the breed specific characteristics and needs.

Herding

Originally, they were bred to help farmers with moving livestock – sheep, cattle, horses and other farm animals. A herding dog is characterised by its herd drive, which is a complex instinct to move the animals in a group. A herding dog uses eye contact, stalking or circling movements, sideways steps and a combination of gestures to move the livestock into specific areas. Typically, this group of dogs are highly energetic, intelligent and often love to work. If you have a family with children, a dog from this group is great because it will work to protect the family, but can also be very energetic and playful in the middle of playtime.

Famous breeds

- **Border Collie**
- **German Shepherd**
- **Cane Corso**
- **Australian Shepherd**
- **Beauceron**
- **Bergamasco Sheepdog**
- **Pembroke Welsh Corgis**

If you do not want to see destructive behaviour, you need to remember with such an energetic dog that you will have to find ways to mentally and physically stimulate them.

For example, at home you can ask your dog to perform simple commands and tricks to make it feel useful. If you have a backyard, you can take your dog for a walk together and have a game of fetch in the yard. These activities will help your herding dog not feel frustrated and burn some of that energy.

Note that not all herding dog breeds are used only for herding. Breeds such as the German Shepherd or Belgium Malinois are popular police and military dogs because of their high levels of intelligence and physical and mental strength.

Sporting

Originally, they were bred to hunt specific species of prey, birds or larger mammals like deer and boar. They are referred to as hunting dogs. Their exceptional endurance characterises sporting dogs, high energy, skilled swimmers, intelligent with a love for the outdoors. Their coat has adapted to be water repellent and to help them keep warm when the temperature is cold. This group of dogs are great for active families who love outdoor adventures. They are friendly and loyal. It's worth pointing out that they can develop stubbornness if not properly trained.

Famous breeds

- **English Cocker Spaniel**
- **Irish Setter**
- **Labrador Retriever**
- **Golden Retriever**
- **German Shorthaired Pointer**
- **Weimaraner**
- **Brittany**

If you are interested in owning a dog from this group, you should have a large garden and be prepared to take your dog for a few walks per day. It is not uncommon for sporting dogs to wear out their owners before themselves, as they have high stamina.

To prevent behaviour issues with a dog from this group, you need to introduce variety into their day. Don't expect a short, clean and normal walks. Such dogs will want to run, chase, retrieve, swim and more. Give your dog agility, tracking or obedience training – activities that require high levels of energy and mental stimulation.

Today, besides being used for hunting, this group is one of the most popular for modern dog jobs such as service dogs (guide dogs, diabetes alert dog, hearing dogs), therapy dogs, detection dogs, and search and rescue dogs.

Hound

Originally, they were bred to hunt small game like rabbits, hares and foxes. Their exceptional sense of smell characterises them, and it is their primary driver that forms their character. These dogs have a high chase drive, high energy, intelligence and independent nature. Hound dogs are great for owners who live in remote areas, or noise does not bother their neighbours, because they howl or bay when they hear noises, especially at night, which can be disturbing for the household and the neighbours. This group is not recommended for families with small children as they can be overaggressive or shy, with a tendency to be stubborn and aloof with strangers – but loyal with the family.

Famous breeds

- **Basset Hound**
- **Beagle**
- **Dachshund**
- **Bloodhound**
- **Greyhound**
- **Grand Basset Griffon Vendeen**
- **Basenji**

When you are getting a dog from the hound group, you need to make sure that you have a secure fence around your property and lots of toys. Hounds need lots of time with them, as they are social and love to be around humans and other dogs. If you do not give them enough attention, they can become lonely, depressed, and destructive.

Because of their sound sense of smell and chase, you need to be careful on off-leash walks, as they might run away. To prevent this, you need to stimulate them with scent work games around the house and the garden, fetch and lots of walks.

Commonly, this group is used for detection work in police force because of their powerful sense of smell and keen instincts.

Working

Originally, they were bred to work in teams of dogs pulling carts or sledges and work as watchdogs for homes and flocks. The group of breeds includes one of the most ancient dog breeds and is known for strength, courage and stability. Because of their size, they can intimidate, and they are not always suited to families with young children, but they are great with other dogs and fit well in the family unit. A working dog needs a strong owner who can give it respect and discipline. These dogs are magnificent for owners who live in rural areas because they are suited to living outdoors.

Famous breeds

- **Boxer**
- **Rottweiler**
- **Great Dane**
- **Tibetan Mastiff**
- **Siberian Huskies**
- **Alaskan Malamutes**
- **Newfoundland**

This group is great for families who enjoy outdoor activities as they love and benefit to take part in them too. These gentle giants require a lot of time for exercise, attention, and socialisation. It's important to know that big breeds like that have shorter lifespans.

A working dog needs to be trained for obedience, agility and tracking, and you can also give it a sense of having a job by putting a doggy backpack or teaching it how to sledge and having it sledge around the garden.

Today, working dogs continue to assist humans. For example, we often use Newfoundland dogs as therapy dogs or search and rescue dogs.

Terrier

Originally, they were bred to be tenacious, fearless hunters and vermin exterminators. This group is active, playful and energetic, with a strong sense of curiosity. Their small size, short coats and independent traits characterised terriers. These dogs make great friends but also are stubborn and aloof, and they are not suited to owners with young children because of their high energy, they often are overprotective of their territory and can be very vocal. This group is great for owners who live in the country with sizeable gardens or on farms where the dogs can roam freely without being locked up all the time.

Famous breeds

- **Scottish Terrier**
- **Staffordshire Bull Terrier**
- **Jack Russell Terrier**
- **Bull Terrier**
- **Cairn Terrier**
- **Australian Terrier**
- **Rat Terrier**

Don't be fooled by their smaller size, terriers are tough and strong dogs, able to withstand heavy physical activity and last for long periods of time. A terrier needs lots of time with you and should have plenty of toys to keep it occupied, as it can be destructive when left on its own for too long.

Terriers, like other hunting dog breeds, can develop high prey drive, which makes them chase things and feel fear and anxiety towards strangers. They need a lot of training and socialisation from early in life to prevent these behaviour issues.

Today, we use terriers as guard and watchdog animals but also as therapy dogs in hospitals, nursing homes and elderly care facilities.

Toy

Originally, they were bred to be lapdogs in royal courts and entertain people. The group is characterised by its small size, shorter coats, high energy and playful nature. What makes this group different from the rest of the dogs is that these dogs are more reserved towards strangers, but that does not mean they will not socialise with them. Most toy breeds are very loyal and loving towards their family and need plenty of time with their human counterparts and exercise daily, however much less compared to bigger dogs who are used to working all for long hours at a time.

Famous breeds

- **Pomeranian**
- **Chihuahua**
- **Pug**
- **Yorkshire Terrier**
- **Cavalier King Charles Spaniel**
- **Pekingese**
- **Bichon Frisé**

Most common behaviour issues for untrained toy dogs are excessive barking, separation anxiety, destructive behaviour and being shy with strangers. All of these can be prevented with proper socialisation and training.

Toy dogs make great indoor pets or city pets, as they can live well within small spaces. Because toy breeds are sometimes very active and have high energy levels, provide them with plenty of toys for them to chew on or play with for extended periods of time.

Toy breeds such as Pomeranians have sensitive ears which can become damaged by loud sounds, so it's important to train your dog early on how to be quiet indoors.

Non-Sporting

This group of dogs generally doesn't fall within the six original groups and is known for its versatility and intelligence. The group includes different dog breeds, of different sizes and temperaments, including working dogs in pastures, guard dogs, rescue dogs and companion dogs. You can think of non-sporting dogs as a "catch-all" group - a variety of dog breeds that are not suitable for the other groups. With being said that all these breeds are great family pets and very sociable.

Famous breeds

- **Chow Chow**
- **Dalmatian**
- **American Bulldog**
- **Poodle**
- **Shiba Inu**
- **French Bulldog**
- **American Eskimo Dog**

Most of this group are very calm and often don't bark unless they feel someone is attacking their territory. (Shiba Inu would be an exception, as these dogs are in a league of their own.). In this group, you will find both couch potato type of dogs and active ones. The ones that are more active just need plenty of time with their humans, both physically and mentally.

Just because non-sporting dogs can't be categorised, it does not mean these dogs are any less special. Some of these dogs are one of the most intelligent breeds and would require plenty of mental stimulation, as with any other intelligent dog.

Today, poodles are quite popular for mixing with other breeds, so that the designer breed has the characteristics of a poodle - adorable curly coat that gives little to no shedding, intelligence, and friendly temperament - but with a combination of the second breed it was mixed with, like "Labradoodle."

CHAPTER
FOUR

DOG
AGES &
Stages

DOG
LIFE **Stages**

Just like humans, dogs go through different life stages, which bring a series of changes in their behaviour, needs and interests. When deciding on the right dog for your family, as each stage requires a different approach to training and care.

Depending on the breed and the size of the dog, the duration of each stage and the behaviour of your dog during that stage can vary widely. Think about these variables when you are deciding, as they can have an important impact on your dog's overall development.

PUPPY

Goes up to six months

- Sense development
- Joints and bones are still in development
- Learning and socialisation stage
- Eats three to four times a day

ADOLESCENT

Begins between six to eighteen months

- Hormones kick in
- Starts to push the boundaries and disobey everything they have learned
- Eats three times a day

ADULT

Begins eighteen months to three years

- Reaches full size
- Energy level starts to normalise
- You can continue mental and physical stimulations
- Eats two times a day

SENIOR

It can begin between seven to ten years

- Starts getting grey hairs
- Requires more sleep
- Requires calmer walks
- Joint and health problems might occur

It is almost impossible to accurately predict your dog's behaviour in any one particular life stage, although there are some typical behaviours that you might observe and general guidelines that can help.

Each of the life stages is covered in more detail in the next pages, as I've focused mostly on puppyhood and adolescence as these are the biggest changes you will observe and where you will need to spend the most time with your pup training and guiding it to become it's best self.

PUPPY

If you are getting your dog as a puppy, you should not be getting it earlier than eight weeks because before that it's crucial for its physical and mental development to be with its mum and litter. During that stage, their senses develop, their personality, and they learn crucial socialisation skills and cues.

A vivacious and curious puppy needs to be kept busy and entertained. This stage usually lasts for about six months. Puppies grow quickly during this time.

Growth

- Bones and joints are still forming.
- Weight doubles the first two months.
- Teething starts.
- They have a small bladder.

Sleep

Puppies sleep eighteen to twenty hours a day, as this is the only time they release their growth hormone. Since puppies wake up several times a night, it's important to get them used to sleeping in their own beds as soon as possible.

Health and Care

- It should be weaned at eight weeks.
- Dogs should not be de-sexed at this age.
- It should have its first vet visit.
- By eighteen weeks, it should have all its first vaccines and parasite treatments.

Exercise

As your pup's joints are developing is important not to over exercise your new furry friend. If you do that, you can not only damage its musculoskeletal development, but you can end up with joint problems later in life. Keep the walks short and calm, no longer than fifteen minutes and no excessive running.

Nutrition

When you pick up your pup, it's preferable to continue with the food it was given. You can gradually change it; however, it needs to be puppy and growth support specific, as it will help with their nutritional and growth needs. If you change it drastically, they will get an upset stomach. Feeding should be three times a day to prevent sugar drops in the blood system. At this stage, it is normal for pups to eat more.

Mental Development

As part of their physical growth, puppies develop mentally and explore more. Often this stage is called "The Fear Stage" because puppies become afraid of things such as new people, dogs or environments. As discussed in the training and socialisation chapter, it's essential you desensitise them, but gradually, and do not push them. This is a very crucial time for a puppy's mental development, as you will develop their confidence in the future and prevent behaviour issues.

Puppy Training During Eight to Twelve Weeks

Training starts from the first day but with simple requests. Its name, the house rules, leash training and the most basic commands – yes, okay, no, sit, stay and down. Go slowly. At this stage, your pup will be very excitable and food motivated. Use this time to build trust and respect in your relationship.

Puppy Training During Three to Six Months

At this age, the pup has better control of its bladder and bowels, which means it will start sleeping through the night and the potty training will pay off, if it hasn't already.

At sixteen weeks, you might notice your dog has increased fearfulness, which is completely normal. The best way to deal with it is to avoid overwhelming your dog and ignore the behaviour, not reward it.

As your dog is nearing adolescence, you notice it will test the boundaries, and this is where you need to keep up with the house rules and the training. If you want to join a puppy training class, it's a perfect time, as all the vaccinations are done and it's not at risk of catching a disease.

To help with teething, provide plenty of chew toys to allow safe chewing.

ADOLESCENT

Welcome to the teenager stage of puppyhood. We know this stage for being the most difficult time for both dogs and handler. If inappropriate behaviour wasn't corrected, it is easier to correct as an adult, as this is where even the best-behaved pup will push your boundaries and disobey. You need to be patient with your pup in this stage, like you would every teenager. They go through changes which make it hard for them to control their emotions.

Growth

- Growth will slow down.
- Small breeds will almost reach their full size.
- Medium and larger breeds have a few more months to grow.
- It should have all its teeth at this point.

Health and Care

- Smaller dogs can be neutered after six months.
- Medium dogs can be neutered after eighteen months.
- When it reaches one-year, top-up vaccinations.
- Your dog should have monthly flea and tick treatments.
- Your dog should be dewormed every three months.

Sleep

Sleep hours decrease; however, they still need from fourteen to sixteen hours of sleep at this stage.

Exercise

As the puppy reaches adolescence, it's important to keep exercise low to medium intensity. A good way to plan the length of your walks is, for every month they are up to five minutes of exercise two to three times a day. For example, a seven-month-old pup can have up to a thirty-five-minute walk at a time.

Nutrition

At around twelve months, you can start switching to adult food and feeding can go down to two times a day. The number of treats you give throughout the day should be considered when calculating their calories, and their meals should reflect this. At around twelve months, your dog's calorie needs will also decrease, as they are no longer growing. However, for medium and large breeds, the extra calories will continue to be needed until eighteen to twenty-four months. After neutering your dog, you will need to reduce the calories by another ten percent.

Mental Development

You will notice that your pup will have an increase in energy and independence and will exhibit more destructive behaviour. It's good to continue to socialise your pup. Even if the most important socialisation period has finished, they continue to grow their confidence and explore the world.

Don't allow inappropriate behaviour and assume that automatically your pup will grow out of it, you have to ensure to prevent and redirect it every time, else it will become a pattern and a habit, which is much harder to correct.

Puberty Signs in Males

- Beginning of raising its leg to pee
- Testicular descent
- Increase interest in roaming and disinterest in commands and cues
- Beginning to "mark" its territory
- May show aggression towards other males
- May run after other dogs
- Starts to hump dogs and other objects
- May begin to resource guard
- Increased lack of focus, concentration and respect
- Increased destructive behaviour

Puberty Signs in Females

- Beginning of heat cycle that comes with increased urination and licking in the area, and red discharge
- May show aggression towards males during heat
- May be lethargic
- May begin to show unpredictable behaviour
- May begin to resource guard
- Increased lack of focus, concentration and respect
- Increased destructive behaviour

Training During Six to Eighteen Months

Training during puberty is the most challenging time, where a lot of owners give up, but if you give up, you risk creating long-term behaviour problems with your pup.
You will notice a drop in the commands you thought were mastered. This is normal. Be patient, consistent and firm. Continue with the training sessions, and reinforce the same commands and add new ones. Keep using the treats. It is still too early to remove them from the training. Always, always set your commands for success, as you do not want your pup to think it can choose when to perform a command or not, and do not repeat commands after your dog. The house accidents should be next to zero, but if they happen, do not punish but assess why they happen. Did you leave your dog unattended, or did you skip the morning walk?

ADULT

Congratulations on reaching adulthood with your pup. Depending on your dog's size, this could be about twelve months or twenty-four months. You should see a lot of your pup's best behaviour, where your pup is well-trained and follows the house rules, while any destructive behaviour will be limited. House accidents should be zero or at least, very rare. You can start allowing more freedom in the house and trusting them to stay unsupervised for longer periods (accumulating these freedoms, of course).

Health and Care

Your dog will only require yearly check ups and it's monthly treatments, unless there has been an accident or another need.

Sleep

As a fully grown adult dog, it will sleep on average between eleven to fourteen hours.

Nutrition

Once your dog has reached full size, and it's been neutered, it will require much less food. There should be no need for supplements unless advised otherwise by your vet.

Exercise

These are the most active years of your dog's life. For most breeds, at least sixty minutes per day of exercise is required to keep them happy. (At least!) In most cases more. You can take them on trips, for runs or to the beach, and your dog will be happy and have the energy to do so.

Training

Yes, your dog will stop pushing boundaries and by adulthood should have a good grasp, if not mastered, all the basic commands. However, the training doesn't need to stop at basic. Most dogs love to train and will thank you for being mentally stimulated.

Why stop there? Build on the skills they already have and continue to challenge them, adding more distractions, longer commands and positions, and more challenges.

SENIOR

You are too far away from your dog's golden years to think ahead, but here are a few points of things you should consider. Depending on the breed and size, your dog might reach its senior years at six to twelve years. Your pet has been your loyal friend for a long time, and now it will need your support and understanding as it ages and it is the final stage of its life.

Signs of aging

- You will notice grey hairs.
- Dental problems may occur.
- Joint problems may occur.
- Senses may decline.
- Mental status may decline.
- Irritability is possible, often caused by pain or discomfort from an undetected condition.
- Your dog may slow down.
- Your dog may experience stiffness.

Nutrition

You will notice your dog's appetite will decrease, and its metabolism will slow. Reduce your dog's portions and feed it two to three times a day. You will need to change to senior labelled food to support its nutritional needs and perhaps start adding supplements for joints or other breed-specific problems.

Sleep

A senior dog requires more sleep, from eighteen to twenty hours per day.

Exercise

Your dog's energy will decrease, and it might have some health issues that will prevent it from being as active as before. That said, you should still give it at least thirty minutes of exercise per day, and it should be low impact. Increase the number of walks and decrease the time of the walk, like three times a day twenty minutes each, rather than two times thirty minutes. The duration of the walk you can have with a senior dog depends on the size, energy and health of your dog.

Special Needs

Be patient with your best friend, as it might forget or not hear a command that used to be always on cue. Its bladder might not be as strong and might to hold as long as before. As your dog ages, you might notice that it's no longer able to climb into the car or the couch alone, so it will need extra hands. Your dog bed will need to be padded to help reduce the risk of joint problems or pain if there are such already. And finally, pay attention to your dog's body language. Don't delay vet visits. Keep them regular, so to get the best advice for your dog and its conditions (if it has any).

CHAPTER
FIVE

DOG
BODY LANGUAGE &
Emotions

DOG
FIVE Senses

Look at your dog. What does it know about the world? How does it learn it? Your paw friend uses its five senses to survive in the world. Although there are some key differences between human and canine senses, they also have some similarities.

Just like humans, when dogs use all of their senses together at the same time, they are in a state known as "synaesthesia." Using a combination of all five senses at once, dogs can learn about the world around them at a much faster rate than if they used only two or three of them at once.

Some dog breeds have special abilities. For example, some breeds can smell gases in the air for miles. Though, dogs use all of their senses to learn about the world around them. Dogs use their senses to explore, learn about their environment, find food, to hunt and to feel safe.

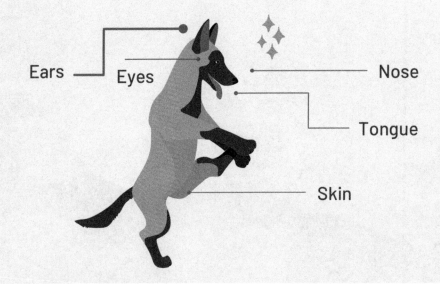

Ears

Eyes

Nose

Tongue

Skin

What Do They Do?

To see   To hear   To smell   To touch   To taste

Sight

Dogs have great eyesight. They can see some colour and can also see well in low light. Dogs have a binocular field of view of 180 degrees, the same as humans, which means they can judge distance and depth very well. Despite this ability, dogs' vision isn't as quite as ours.

Even though dogs peripheral vision is nearly 300 degrees on either side, and can take in almost everything around them at once, it is not as clear as humans, as their eyes are set wider apart. Meaning, peripherally, they don't pick up minor details as well as us, but will notice movements in the surroundings. However, dog's vision is exceptionally sharp and is much better than humans, near the centre of their visual field.

Seeing-eye dogs can see things that are very far away; their vision is believed to be four times stronger at night than in humans.

Sound

Hearing creates soundwaves in their heads that are then picked up by their ears. Dogs have a good sense of hearing. They have a wide range of frequencies. They can hear higher and lower notes than humans (20,00Hz). This includes sounds from 47 kilohertz to 67,000 kilohertz.

Smell

Smell is one of the most important senses for dogs. They can smell prey that is buried underground, detect disease in people and animals, and find their way back home after being lost. Dogs use their sense of smell to tell where other dogs are, how old they are, and how healthy they are.

Dogs have about twenty times as many smell-sensitive cells in their noses as people do. The area in the dog's brain that recognises smells is greater than ours too. We can train dogs to recognise certain odours, such as the scent of cancer or chemicals from land mines buried underground.

Touch

Dogs have an amazing sense of touch. A dog's sense of touch is about five times greater than humans. Their sense of touch is so acute, they can even sense vibrations through the ground. This helps them know approximately the size and speed of an object coming near them.

Taste

Dogs have 1700 taste buds, which is fewer than us. Dogs cannot taste sweet things or bitter things, but they can detect sour flavours.

CAN DOGS
SEE ANY Colour?

The short answer is yes. The longer answer is that, although dogs are in fact not colour blind, they only see a limited range of colours. So, technically speaking, dogs have a few colours they can differentiate from one another.

Humans

Red, blue, and green combinations can be recognised by three types of cones in human eyes, which allow us to see colours brighter and recognise more combinations and shades.

Dogs

Unlike humans, dogs can only discern blue and yellow colours. We know this as dichromatic vision.

What does it mean for you?

Basically, a dog's world comprises shades of blue, yellow and grey with no red, green or orange colours. The yellow and blue toys will make the most impression on your dog, while anything red will most likely go unnoticed.

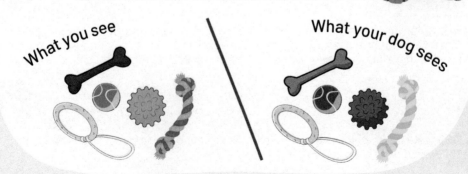

What you see

What your dog sees

NATURAL DOG BEHAVIOURS
AND HOW TO
Redirect Them

In the same way, as your dog's motivators are largely based on its breed, you find that for the best part of your dog's natural behaviours have been bred into it for generations. For example, we breed beagles to be hunters, and instinctively they will chase, especially after smells.

As an owner, you cannot expect your dog not to be a dog. It is simply not possible, and any efforts will make everyone involved miserable. Instead, understand why your dog has the urge to dig or rip things apart and provide a safe alternative.

Redirecting natural behaviour that can turn destructive is actually quite easy. First, observe what your dog's tendencies are and then try to replicate them with enrichment activities.

Let's say you have a Labrador, and it has the tendency to chew and shred things apart. Provide your dog with a toy they can do that to. You can even give your dog a job and ask it to rip and shred your empty delivery boxes. Believe me, it will make your dog so happy to feel included and to be allowed to shred, and also you will have to do less work when filling your recycling bin.

Learn more about enrichment activities in chapter ten, page 196.

Most common natural behaviours

1. Chewing and shredding
2. Running
3. Digging
4. Barking
5. Howling
6. Whining
7. Scent marking
8. Sniffing
9. Retrieving
10. Licking

You will notice that your dog will behave better overall when allowed to follow its natural instincts safely. As a result, your pooch will be less destructive and more relaxed, and you will have more fun with your best friend.

KEY BODY LANGUAGE SIGNS
YOUR DOG WANTS YOU To Know

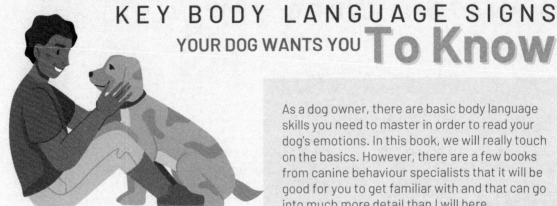

As a dog owner, there are basic body language skills you need to master in order to read your dog's emotions. In this book, we will really touch on the basics. However, there are a few books from canine behaviour specialists that it will be good for you to get familiar with and that can go into much more detail than I will here.

Dogs are not only unable to communicate verbally, but they also don't communicate with their hands and arms the way humans do. Thus, you have to observe their whole body to read what they are feeling.

What to look for in your dog when identifying its emotions

1. Tail Wagging

Tail wagging doesn't always mean happiness and eagerness

In fact, sometimes it can be a sign of pain, nerviness, trouble or even aggression. You need to observe where is the tail located and how big are the wags. For example, if the tail is low, and the wags are short and fast, then it's probably a sign of submissive or nervous emotions.

More details on how to recognise the basic emotions on page 73

2. Ear Movement

Whether your dog has floppy or pointy ears, its movement and position can also be an indicator of the dog's feelings. If the ears are pointing forward, but the dog isn't moving them, he is alert to something, especially if the mouth is closed.

3. Mouth

Is your dog's jaw relaxed or tensed, is your dog licking its lips, or is the tongue sitting down? Licking lips and can mean two different things, depending on the context.

The first situation could be, you are hugging your dog and getting into its personal space. The first thing it does is tense its body and turn its head away from you, then licks. What does this mean? Your dog is nervous, as it's not happy about this invasion.

In the second situation, you are making a sandwich, and your dog is sitting with a puppy's eye looking up to you whilst licking its lips. Is it nervous? Of course not. It's licking its lips because it wants your food. This is a great example of how the same movement would mean different things in the situation's context.

4. Eyes

Are the eyes relaxed or hard? Do you see the whites of your dog's eyes, or are the lids sitting heavy? If you see the whites of your dog's eyes, something is bothering it, but again, it has to be read in the full picture. Ears pointing forward, but the dog isn't moving them, it is alert to something, especially if the mouth is closed.

5. Position of Its Body

Is your dog turning on its back and exposing its belly, or have its tail between its legs, or maybe your dog's head is down? Is your dog jumping up or hiding behind you? All these body movements combined with their facial expression will paint the full picture.

Relaxed

Dogs with relaxed mouths – might be slightly open but not necessary – slitted eyelids, soft eyes, no tension in the ears and forehead. There should be little or no movement in the tail of your dog, and you shouldn't be able to see the whites of its eyes.

Playful

Everyone should be able to tell the difference between a relaxed dog and a playful, cheerful dog. Your dog will have its tail up and will most likely wag, its mouth will be open and it will resemble a smile or grin, its eyes will be open and sparkly, and it will bring you a toy to play with.

Alert

When alert, your dog's ears will be up and forward, neck will be straight, head will be held high, mouth will be closed, and its eyes will be bright and focused. Your dog's body will be in an easy to move position and will wait in anticipation for what is next. It may become alert before a command, if they see another animal to chase, or if they hear a distant sound.

Anxious

When a dog is anxious or nervous, but not quite afraid, you might notice tensing of the body and it may search for a way to release it. It might look in the following ways - avoiding eye contact, having wide eyes, yawning, licking lips, shaking their head, having flattened and moving ears, having tension in the forehead, lowering bodies, and sometimes a low quick wagging of the tail.

Fearful

When your dog is afraid, you will see the white of its eyes, and they will be wide open and moving rapidly to observe the situation. It will search to cover its body, its tail will be between its legs or low, and it will try to hide behind you or another subject with its ears flattened. Some dogs will growl, bark, and some might roll on their backs, or freeze and shut down by not responding to any stimuli. Whenever you notice a drastic and change in your dog's behaviour, try to remove them from the situation as soon as possible.

Vulnerable

In situations involving new dogs or people, you might notice your dog will become more submissive than usual and exposes its body. Dogs do that to show their belly and make themselves look smaller to another dog or human. They will lower their bodies, back legs, tail and sometimes their ears.

Angry

Most obvious emotion to recognise – bared teeth, growling, hard and focused eyes, hardly blinking, and lunging forward and stiffening its body. Its fur will stand, and the ears will flatten.

Sad

Your dog will be more tired, and the eyes may appear sloppy and squinty. It will not engage in games, and its appetite will change. You might notice excessive licking of its paws, hiding and avoiding everyone. Later on, we will discuss what can make your dog sad and what to do in that case.

Tired

You might notice suddenly more yawning, panting, and licking. Also, your dog may disengage with you and won't respond to commands. It will seek to lie down or hide if it's a busy place. Sometimes, it might get hyper and start having zoomies, just like children.

Curious

We have all seen our dogs when they tilt their heads to one side. This is a sign that they are curious about what is going on, and they're trying to assess and process it. It could be when waiting for more instructions from its trainer or when listening to a sound that they are trying to determine its source.

Annoyed

Yes, your dog can get annoyed with you. The signs would be the following: walking away from you, avoiding eye contact or staring at you, giving you the side eye, avoiding physical contact, flattening ears, and sometimes growling. Observe for yawning, licking of lips, closing and tightening lips, showing white of their eyes, stiffened body, or hiding under or behind furniture. Sometimes, you might notice they pee on something of yours on purpose. It can be a sign, especially if your dog has not had an accident since it was a pup.

Aroused

This would be when your dog gets hyper because of its favourite things. It will jump up , it might open its mouth, ears are forward, tail is up and wagging, body is straight and stiff, eyes are focused. I might pair it with barking, whining, spinning and pacing.

WHY DO
DOGS GET THE
Zoomies?

Let's start with the obvious question first, what are zoomies? Zoomies are when your dog gets a sudden burst of energy and starts running around at full speed. Additionally, they might bark and jump. Zoomies are mostly seen in young, untrained dogs. As a dog gets older and more well-behaved, the zoomies usually go away or become an occasional thing.

01 Bored

When your dog has been bored for a long period and has used little of its energy, it is highly likely that the smallest excitement can trigger a zoomie attack.

Tired 02

Just like children, dogs can get hyper when tired and suddenly start running around at full speed.

03 Stressed

Stress is a factor that can trigger a zoomie attack, especially noticed if we forced them to do something they don't enjoy – like taking a bath, their nails being cut, or the hoover was on.

Aroused 04

Zoomies are also triggered by something interesting happening, like when you come home from work and greet your dog, or when you give it a new toy to play with, or they see a puddle and they can run in off the lead.

05 After eating

Just like children, after eating you might notice your dog gets really hyper from the sudden increase of sugar. It's good to try to prevent this, as running on a full stomach can cause digestion problems.

IS YOUR DOG
Reactive?

You first need to understand that there is a difference between a reactive dog and an aggressive dog. In both cases, it is best to seek a dog behaviourist to help you understand and deal with the triggers for your dog.

A reactive dog is triggered by stimuli, and it is not an aggressive dog; however, it might escalate if not handled properly. The stimuli might trigger different emotions – excitement, fear or danger, depending on the level of the stimuli and the past experience of your dog in these trigger situations.

An angry dog is often reacting to a trigger of its fight-or-flight response because it's feeling threatened.

Observe your dog's body language. Is it barking or growling? Is its body stiff? Can you see the white of its eyes? In the previous pages, I've explained the signs of a stressed, anxious and angry dog.

What can make your dog reactive?

01 Poor socialisation

I repeat in this book time and time again the importance of proper socialisation, especially in the first three to six months of your pup's life. These experiences will form your dog's confidence and experience of the world.

Past experience 02

If you are getting a rescue dog, unfortunately, you cannot help what they have been through before you, and often you might not even know. If your dog has had a traumatising past, you will have to be patient with it and work with professionals to help bring its confidence and trust back.

03 Untreated conditions that cause your dog pain

Just like humans, when your dog is in pain, it will be more irritable and it also feels more vulnerable. If your dog is in pain, avoid putting it in situations that might become triggers.

Backyard breeders 04

If your pup's mum has carried the pups and raised them in unfavourable conditions, the stress hormones, the lack of nutrition and her health issues are likely to be carried down to her litter.

TRIGGERS

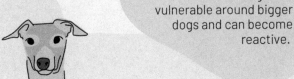

Every other dog

Your dog might simply want to play with every dog and pull and lunge for that.

Big dogs

Smaller dogs feel vulnerable around bigger dogs and can become reactive.

Specific dogs

They had an unpleasant experience in the past, like being attacked or being bitten.

Other people

They had a poor experience or poor exposure.

Leash

Your dog was trained incorrectly or had a poor experience in the past.

Food

Resource guarding can start when someone is trying to take food away from your dog or tries to play with your dog while it's eating.

Toys

Your dog is resource guarding, if your dog is snatching them from other dogs or children

Bikes and skateboards

They can startle your dog, especially if it is not used to them.

Dog park

Your dog is not used to large numbers of other dogs and potential attacks.

Certain sounds

Your dog could be bothered by thunder or fireworks, for example.

WHAT TO DO IF YOUR DOG IS TRIGGERED?

01   Do not touch your dog.

02   Get as far away as possible from the trigger.

03   Take control of the situation and give them a command to focus on.

04   Give your dog space.

05   Turn a negative experience into a positive.

06   Contact a dog behaviourist for further advise

Aggressive and reactive behaviour do not develop overnight and will not be cured overnight. It takes time – at least four to six weeks – to see whether your dog's behaviour is improving, but it takes much longer to go from reactive or aggressive back to being a stable and confident dog. So be patient and seek help.

BE PATIENT, AND SEEK HELP.

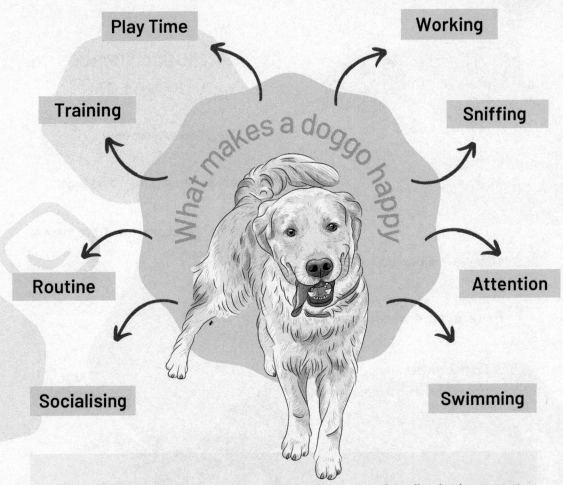

Play Time

Working

Training

Sniffing

Routine

Attention

Socialising

Swimming

What makes a doggo happy

A dog's happiness shines through, as our canine companions live in the present moment. Activities where they are mentally and physically stimulated, such as training, exercising, swimming, playing and socialising, are sure-fire ways for your dog to be in its happy place.

Although some dog breeds can adjust to a changing schedule, most thrive in a routine. Routine gives them a sense of security, and knowing what they will eat, when they will walk, and what food they will get are examples of routines.

As most dogs are pack animals, having the comfort of companionship and knowing where they fit in with their family is vital to a dog's overall happiness. One of the best ways you can show your dog that you love it is by making sure you spend time together.

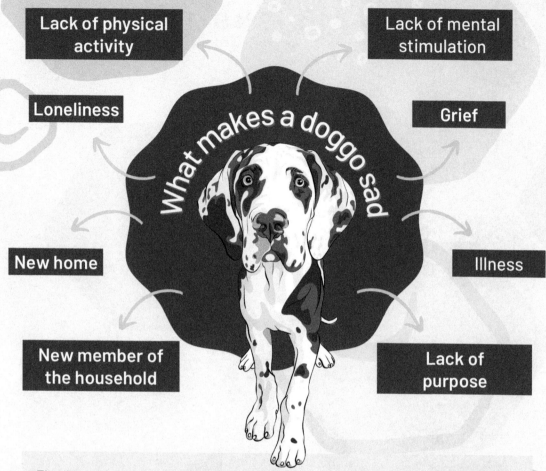

Lack of physical activity

Lack of mental stimulation

Loneliness

What makes a doggo sad

Grief

New home

Illness

New member of the household

Lack of purpose

The things that make your dog sad are like those that make humans sad. There is no doubt that your pup can get upset and jealous when you bring a new pet or a baby. Similarly, if you change the home you have lived in for years, you might expect a temporary change of mood. Remember that neglecting your dog by ignoring their needs, such as exercise, training and quality time, will affect their mood.

Your dog is a lot more than just a furry pet. They can sense when you're feeling down, and they want to make sure that their human feels better too! In fact, dogs are very much like a member of the family. They feel your emotions and grief for lost members.

The good news is that dogs rarely fall into clinical depression and need medication to improve their mood. If you are patient and give them love and attention, most cases will resolve themselves.

SIGNS THAT YOUR PUPPY IS Bored

Pacing

Hyper behaviour

Destructive behaviour - digging, chewing, scratching

Running away

Barking or whining

Sleeping all the time

Panting

Obsessive behaviour

Following you around

A bored puppy can quickly become sad or destructive. Even a well-trained grown dog will not behave if it is bored.

HOW TO PREVENT
PUPPY
Boredom ?

Training

Playing games

Enrichment activities

Take them to new parks for their walks

Enforce daily routine

Ensure proper daily exercise

Interactive toys

Consider dog classes

If you have tried anything to keep your dog physically and mentally entertained and continue to observe abnormal behaviours, speak with a vet and a pet behaviourist for help, as it might be an entirely different problem.

DOG'S DIFFERENT
Motivators

Depending on your dog's breed, one thing might motivate your dog more than another. Labradors, for example, love food and affection, whereas terriers might enjoy a game of chase. Depending on the breed's physical ability and personality, one dog might have more than one motivator. What your dog enjoys will largely determine what your dog loves to do, like are they bred to hunt, to herd, to track? What is their natural drive? Once you discover this, you will be much closer to finding your pup's motivators.

Now, why do you need to understand your dog's motivators?

Because when you train your dog, you ensure your dog knows that if it listens to you, it will receive a high-value reward.

Else, especially when it reaches the teenager's phase, it will stop listening to you, as what you are offering is not of much importance to your pup.

Food

It's the most common motivator and the easiest to use. If your dog stops listening to you, stop feeding it from its bowl and feed it by hand with commands.

Praise

Most dogs love when they please their owners and are easily pleased by simple praise. However, younger dogs' praise is not always enough, and it needs to be backed up by more incentives.

Playtime

This is where you have to know your dog well and understand which games are its favourite. Do they love chasing, stalking, tracking, playing with balls, or playing tug-of-war? By understanding the game your dog loves the most, you can use training methods specifically to build this game into a training session.

Toys

Some dogs love squeaky toys, chewing toys or demolishing a toy. Maybe your dog only plays with its toys when it's alone or when you are away. If this is the case, you don't want to rely on the toy as a reward, but on praise or some other high-value reward.

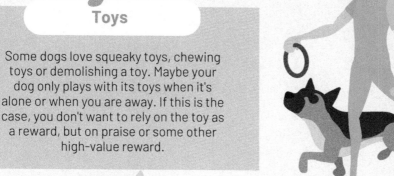

Affection

How much your dog loves attention and affection can carry from its breed and age. Some dogs love cuddling and being petted while others might prefer a game. However, it's usually easy to get your dog to pay attention to you just by giving him some attention. But you need to observe if affection is a motivator for your dog or not.

In order to train your dog effectively, you must recognise the things that drive your pooch. You can turn games into training sessions, feeding times, or even pet time. With this type of training session, I assure you that your dog is learning and having a great time, and you also know that your training is successful.

CHAPTER
SIX

HEALTH
AND
Wellbeing

DOG
HEALTH 101

An annual vet visit isn't enough to ensure your pup is healthy. You can provide your dog with the most beneficial care over its lifetime by following routine preventative care, understanding its breed, scheduling consistent veterinary appointments, and keeping it active with regular exercise.

Here are the most common problems you might encounter during your dog's life and how to react to them and recognise them.

Skin infections

Dog skin can be prone to infection, and the causes can differ from food allergy and pollen allergy to bacterial infection from swimming in dirty waters. If your dog is scratching or licking consistently in the same spot, or you notice sores on your dog, it is best to visit your vet and get diagnosed and given the right treatment.

Dental diseases

Although young dogs tend to not have such problems is best to observe your pup's gums, especially as they are teething. There are some breeds that are prone to dental issues, so it is best to keep an eye open for them. The most common problems are tartar and gingivitis. However, there could be accidents of stuck foreign objects or periodontal diseases. In most of these cases, you need a vet to prescribe the proper treatment and it can vary from simply cleaning the teeth to removing the infected one.

Bad breath, loose teeth, increased drooling, sudden change in temper, refusal to eat and lumps under the tongue are all symptoms of dental disease. Read more on page 103.

Ear infections

Dogs with floppy ears are prone to ear infections and regular cleaning will help prevent ear infections that can cause serious complications, such as deafness, or even result in death if untreated. They can happen from a build-up of dirt, allergies or bacteria.

If your dog's ears are red or you see crusts or scabs and it is scratching its ear, treat it at once. In most cases, a common antibiotic and daily cleaning of the ear will clear it within a week or two. Sometimes, especially if your dog is having them regularly, the vets will like to test the sample to determine what is causing the infection and prescribe more specialised treatment.

Allergies

Dogs have allergies to other things in the environment and their food, which can cause symptoms like sneezing, runny nose, itching eyes and skin irritations. If you suspect your dog has such an allergy, you will need to take it for allergy testing and provide a special diet (a result of the test). Read more about food allergies on page 116.

Cuts

The first cut might make you panic, but over time, like with children, you'll realise how often your dog gets cuts, especially if it's an active dog running free in the woods and fields. Often, all you need to do is disinfect and keep it clean, and the fur will grow back within two to four weeks. If a cut gets infected, you will need to consult your vet and they might prescribe antibiotics. If the wound is deep, it may need stitches.

Digestive disorders

It's quite common for dogs to have upset stomachs that can cause them diarrhoea or vomiting. For most, you don't need to be worried, as it will resolve itself within a couple of days. If you notice your dog has an upset stomach, reduce their activity level and stop any treats and keep them on a plain diet.

Note that if your dog vomits a few times, for more than a day, take it to the vet. If you see in your dog poo blood that might result from haemorrhoids or worse, so consult your vet immediately.

Urinary problems

Urinary problems are usually not serious but can cause your dog discomfort and distress. A urinary tract infection (UTI) is a common infection that is caused by bacteria originating from the mouth, vagina, or anus. Vets will usually prescribe antibiotics and painkillers. If that doesn't help, a urine sample needs to be done to determine the exact bacteria causing the infection.

The most common sign would be if your dog cannot hold it and has accidents in the house, difficult or painful urinating, blood in urine, and increased licking on the genitals.

Kennel cough

This is a contagious disease caused by various bacteria and viruses spread among dogs. If your dog has not been vaccinated and visits a dog park, it is more likely to catch this. It spreads easily through the air and through sneezing, coughing and licking.

Besides coughing, sneezing and running nose, you should not see other symptoms. It's relatively easy to clear up with treatment; however, your dog should be kept separate from other dogs for fourteen days, as in older dogs kennel cough can cause more complications.

Obesity

Obesity is becoming a more common problem with dogs, which causes a variety of health problems, diabetes, arthritis and breathing problems. Although if you keep your dog on a daily walk and offer them exercise, this will not be an issue for you. Most importantly, do not overfeed your dog. Some breeds will continue to eat and act hungry even after they have eaten more than enough.

Stiffness and pain

A variety of conditions can trigger canine stiffness and inflammation. Diseases associated with ageing, such as arthritis and dysplasia often cause inflammation and stiffness, but infestations of parasites and viral or bacterial infections may also be responsible. To prevent or reduce stiffness, your dog should exercise regularly. If your dog is still stiff after spending a few minutes exercising, consult a vet.

Parasites

It is very common for dogs to have parasites, especially those that live on farms or in close proximity to wild animals. Depending on the situation, parasites can cause serious problems and sometimes even death. Using preventative measures, such as parasite control medicine or deworming medicine for dogs, can prevent many of these problems.

Symptoms depend on the type of parasite but can include diarrhoea, vomiting, scooting, weight loss and tiredness. More on page 93.

It's your **responsibility** to watch for **changes** in your dog's behaviour, and if you notice **any**, consult your **vet** immediately. You don't want to wait for the problem to **worsen**.

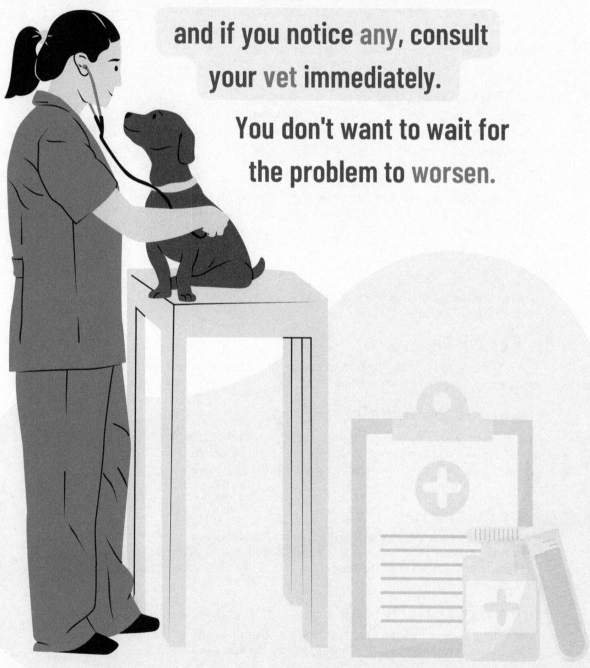

EXTERNAL DOG
Parasites

It is one of the most common problems for canines, especially if you have a dog that loves scavenging and eating on the street. If left untreated, they can cause serious problems, but in most situations, treatments are quite easy and have little effect on your dog. Therefore, early detection and treatment are highly recommended to avoid worsening the situation.

1 Fleas

Fleas are small six-legged parasites that feed on blood. They can cause severe skin infections and provoke allergic dermatitis, as well as other diseases. They can also carry tapeworms.

2 Ticks

Ticks also suck on blood, have eight legs and are slightly larger, with a bulbous shape. They can transmit diseases such as Lyme disease, babesiosis and ehrlichiosis. Their bite is painless, but you can see the tick when it wakes up on the skin.

3 Lice

A louse is a tiny parasite with six muscular legs that attach to hair and feed by biting or sucking blood.

4 Ear Mites

Ear mites are microscopically tiny parasites that feed on ear wax and oils, and cause inflammation and itching.

5 Sarcoptes Scabiei

Highly contagious skin disease that is caused by mites that lay their eggs under the skin and create manifestation and irritation on the skin. The dog will start excessively scratching, which would lead to sores, scabs and even hair loss.

6 Cheyletiella Mites

Small eight-legged mites, that live on the surface of the skin and look like dandruff. However, they are highly contagious and spend their full lifespan (thirty-six days) on the host. They can cause severe skin irritation and hair loss.

7 Demodectic Mange

A long-bodied eight-legged mite that feeds on the oil glands and follicles. They cause intense itching, hair loss, crusting and paw swelling.

External parasites can be caught literally anywhere, even inside your home, as they can come from open doors and windows. External parasites can also bring internal parasites with them, such as Lyme disease by ticks or heartworm larva by mosquitoes.

INTERNAL DOG
Parasites

Vets recommended de-worming treatments (every three months), yearly blood tests for heartworms and tick diseases, and faeces tests for other internal parasites.

Tapeworms 1

Tapeworms usually have no other symptoms, but white grain-like seeds in your dog's faeces. They come from a host like a flea or eating infected raw meat and can't be caught directly by another animal.

Roundworms 2

They are caught by eating or drinking infected water, or faeces, and live free in the intestines. The manifestation can cause vomiting, diarrhoea and weight loss. However, it can be asymptomatic as well.

Hookworms 3

A one- to two-centimetre-long worm that attaches to the lining of the small intestine and feeds on blood. It causes anaemia, which leads to fatigue, pale gums and dull coating.

Whipworms 4

A small worm (six millimetres) that lives inside the large intestine and causes diarrhoea and weight loss. It can be caught by eating dirt or soil contaminated with eggs.

Heartworms 5

A three- to six-inch-long worm that lives in the heart, lungs and blood vessels. It can cause reduced exercise tolerance, coughing, and dyspnoea. It comes from a host such as a mosquito bite that can spread larvae.

Giardia 6

A one cell parasite that attracts the lining of the intestines by absorbing nutrients. The symptoms can be weight loss, low energy, gas and changes in the stool. It can range from a greenish, fatty or watery stool.

Coccidia 7

A small cell organism that can be caught by oocysts in contaminated services. It can cause weakness, loss of appetite, weight loss, and diarrhoea.

Internal parasites are often caught by eating the parasite's eggs, which can be found in faeces, contaminated water, raw contaminated meat, and some plants. Then eggs can then hatch in your dog's stomach and cause a manifestation of symptoms.

VISITS
TO THE VET

It is important to always consult your vet for any concern you might have. A simple phone call where you explain the symptoms can save your dog, or your vet can guide you on how to treat your dog and what to look for.

Some dogs can get anxious if they have a poor experience with a vet, so before you choose your vet, research. Check the reviews, and visit the place in person to see how other dogs and owners feel about it.

If your dog didn't particularly enjoy the examination or the treatment, ensure that you turn the experience to positive with treats, praise and pets.

The first visit usually should be done before you get your puppy, and the vet should do the first set of vaccinations, give the vaccination schedule, and microchip your pup.

When you get your dog, one of the first things you should do is to visit your vet to ensure your dog is healthy and to confirm the vaccination schedule.

First Visit

Yearly Exams

Your vet will perform a routine check-up at your pup's annual exam. This visit can ensure that your dog is in optimal health and may reveal any irregularities early on, before they turn into larger problems.

During this visit, the vet will examine the dog's blood pressure; temperature; respiration rate; heart rate; skin colour and texture; vision, breathing, and aural health; muscle tone; mass or body weight (to see if it has gained or lost weight); as well as teeth and gums. It's recommended to do blood, urine and stool tests in order to catch any issues that might be asymptomatic. You can do the yearly top-up vaccination to protect your pet from the most common canine diseases.

DOG PREVENTATIVE
Treatments

We have all heard it before *"Prevention is better than cure."* With the risk of many diseases and health issues, giving your dog preventative treatments like vaccines and deworming treatments can go a long way in keeping your dog healthy for years and years to come.

VACCINES

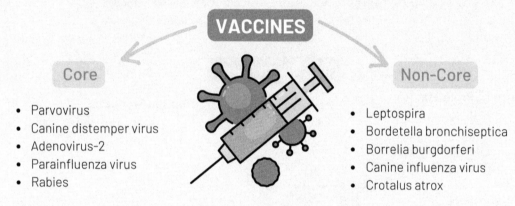

Core

- Parvovirus
- Canine distemper virus
- Adenovirus-2
- Parainfluenza virus
- Rabies

Non-Core

- Leptospira
- Bordetella bronchiseptica
- Borrelia burgdorferi
- Canine influenza virus
- Crotalus atrox

According to AAHA's guidelines, the core vaccines are vital for all puppies and grown dogs, whereas the non-core vaccines are optional. With the non-core vaccines, depending on where you live and the risks that are around you, your vet might recommend them for your dog.

PARASITE PREVENTITIVES

External

- Pill
- Pipette
- Collar

- Pill

Internal

With external parasite prevention, you have a few choices. The most popular is the once-a-month pipette, which you put in between your dog's shoulder blades. Next, you have a collar which you have to change. Note that each brand will last for a different period. Last is the pill, which for some dog owners might be more challenging to give. For the internal parasites, there is only one option - a pill which you will have to give your dog every three months.

TOXIC

NON-EDIBLE ITEMS FOR YOUR  Dog

Some items listed might seem obvious; however, others are not so. Dogs, especially puppies, like exploring the world by chewing. This is a normal part of their development. However, these items can be dangerous for your dog.

If you suspect your dog has eaten something toxic and are unsure what it might be, contact your vet immediately.

Household Items

Cleaning Products:
- Bleach
- Mothballs
- Fabric softener sheets
- Disinfectants

Any medicine

Garden Products:
- Insecticides and pesticides
- Fertilizers
- Weed killers
- Paints

Liquid potpourri

Tobacco

Pool Products:
- Chlorine
- Stabiliser
- Algae Remover

Plastic

Car Products:
- Antifreeze
- Ice Melting Products
- Polish

Poisoning Symptoms

Drooling	Weakness	Rash	Tremors	Abnormal heart beat
Not Eating	Drinking more	Red Skin	Conclusions	Unsteady on feet
Vomiting	Increased urination	Pale gums	Bruising	Agitation
Diarrhoea	Decreased urination	Seizure	Bleeding	Collapse

First, it's a good idea to prepare ahead of time and remove anything your dog might chew in that house. Second, it's important to observe them, and stop them from wandering off and chewing any of these plants.

If you have any of these plants, keep them out of your dog's reach.

Plants

Autumn Crocus
Aloe Vera
Algae
Azalea
Amaryllis
Caster Bean

Cotoneaster
Corn Plant
Cyclamen
Chrysanthemum
Crocuses
Daffodils
Dumbcane
Daphne
Daylily
Dogbane

English Ivy
Foxglove
Garden Star-of-Bethlehem
Gloriosa Lily
Golden Pothos
Grape Vine
Giant Hogweed

Mother-in-Law Tongue
Mistletoe
Mountain Laurel
Oak
Onion and Garlic Plants
Oleander
Peace Lily
Philodendron
Poinsettia

Holly
Horse chestnut
Hyacinths
Hibiscus
Hydrangea
Kalanchoe
Ivy
Lily-of-the-Valley
Laburnum

Potato plants
Pieris Plants
Rowan
Rhubarb Plants
Rhododendron
Rosary Pea
Sago Palm

Schefflera
Stinging Nettle
Tulips
Yesterday, Today Tomorrow Plant
Yew Bush

DO I NEED TO HAVE
MY DOG De-Sexed?

There are loads of misconceptions for neutering or spaying your pet. I get it. I myself was unsure if I wanted to have my dog done or not. But I set out to research. I spoke with specialists and other dog owners who have de-sexed their dogs. I needed to know the pros and cons and to ask about my concerns.

It's a very personal choice whether or not you want to have your dog done. However, when you do make this choice, ensure you are making an educated decision.

MYTHS

It will change my dog's personality.

This is a common misconception; however, de-sexing your puppy will not change its personality. The only thing that may change is their interest in the sex.

My dog will gain weight.

Dogs gain weight from overfeeding and under-exercising, not from neutering or spaying.

It's unnatural.

Yes, it is not, but your dog does not live in the wild - its natural habitat. As a domesticated pet, neutering or spaying is a beneficial procedure.

It's expensive.

Although it is not covered by health insurance, the surgery will cost you less than the treatments your dog might need if you do not de-sex it.

WHEN IS THE RIGHT TIME?

It entirely depends on the size of your dog and the sex of your dog. Larger dogs, as don't stop growing until they are eighteen months old and neutering can affect their growth plates. Smaller dogs can be done after six to eight months as they stop growing earlier.

Female dogs should not be done before their first heat season. Male dogs will show hormonal behaviour signs such as humping, marking and running after female dogs.

Speak with your vet and for your dog breed's specific information to see when is the right time to de-sex them.

AFTERCARE

Ensure its cone is on for ten days to prevent your dog from licking or biting the stitches.

Don't allow the dog to run around for ten days, so the stitches don't open

Observe the stitches for any signs of infection.

Leave your dog in a well ventilated, quiet place to rest and recover from the anaesthetic.

Reduce its calorie intake by ten percent of its regular food to ensure your dog stays a healthy weight.

RISKS IF YOU DON'T GET YOUR DOG DONE

FEMALE

- Can go into heat, which can result in getting pregnant
- Can have some health issues related to being pregnant, however not all
- May become aggressive, especially towards male dogs
- Increased chance of womb infection
- Increased chance of phantom pregnancy
- Increased chance of ovarian cancer

MALE

- Will rush after other dogs, causing them to be attacked
- Will disengage, roaming independently
- Will mark your yard to claim it as his territory
- Some breeds can be aggressive and may attack other dogs
- May get oversexed and hump anything
- Increased prostate diseases
- Increased chance of testicular cancer

BREEDING

Do not assume that before de-sexing, your dog needs to mate once, or experience motherhood once in order to fill fulfilled. Dogs do not feel the loss of their reproductive system, as they don't have a concept of it, and don't know that they can or cannot reproduce. Simply put, it's an instinct driven by their hormones. Therefore, if you are not a professional breeder, I will discourage you from breeding your dog in order to "return your investment from buying a purebred dog".

During COVID lockdown, as the marketing for puppies grew, a lot of inexperienced dog owners started backyard breeding their dogs and selling their pups. This type of breeding is irresponsible, as often mating is not based on the knowledge of the family history of the other dog. The breeder would not know how to handle and treat the mum and the litter, which can lead to many complications for the mother and the puppies in the future.

IDEAL
DOG'S Weight

If you are getting a purebred dog, Kennel Clubs have charts listing the range by breed for male and female dogs. If you have a rescue dog and you don't know the breed, or you have a mix-breed dog, there is still a way to determine if your dog is at a healthy weight.

Vets have a system called BCS (Body Condition System), where your dog's waist, ribs and muscles are visually inspected by a vet. In the USA the system is one through nine, whereas in Europe the point system is one to five.

Critically underweight

- The dog appears bony from afar, and you can feel ribs, spine and hip bones.
- Low muscle mass
- Low to no visible body fat
- An excessively narrow waist

Underweight

- The dog might not appear bony from afar, but you can still feel the ribs and other bones.
- The waist is still quite narrow.
- There is more muscle mass, however, still visibly low.
- It is hard to notice any fat under the skin.

Ideal

- You can feel the ribs, but you can feel the muscle of them.
- You can see the waist behind the ribs.
- The abdomen is line high.
- Muscles are visible.

Overweight

- Difficult to feel the dog's ribs, as fat is covering them.
- The waist can't be seen from above.
- The abdomen line is hanging low.
- May notice fat deposits.

Obese

- Visible fat deposits on the neck, limbs and spine.
- The waist is absent.
- The abdomen is low with no tuck.

DO I NEED TO USE
Supplements

Yes and no. I know, it's not the answer you were searching for, but unfortunately, there is no simple answer, as it depends on a lot of factors that I will explore below.

Why you might **not need it**

Ideally, your dog should not require supplements if it eats a healthy, balanced diet. Like humans, dogs should be able to get all of their vitamins and minerals through their normal diet, unless we are deficient or on a special diet.

We will explore in depth the food and nutritional needs of dogs in the next chapter.

Why you might need it

Multiple reasons may require special attention for some dogs, including digestive disorders, joint or mobility problems, coat or skin problems, and heart or allergy problems. These conditions may require a combination of medication, special food, and supplements to resolve. It's really worth taking your dog to the vet if you think he may have any of these problems, as early intervention with the correct plan can make a tremendous difference.

Supplements are also useful if you want to supplement your puppy's growth or your dog is predisposed to breed specific problems.

Which minerals and vitamins you might want to supplement with?

- Fish oil and flaxseed
- Omega-3 fatty acids
- Vitamin D3, K2, A, C, B
- Calcium

- Probiotics
- Antioxidants
- Choline

It is imperative that you consult your veterinarian before giving any supplements to your dog and to determine the proper dosage based on the dog's current diet and needs. In excess, vitamins and minerals may cause your dog more harm than good.

DOG'S
DENTAL Health

A lack of knowledge results in most dental issues in younger dogs. However, the case is different with older dogs, as they may develop oral problems, particularly those with flat faces. Dental health is a vital part of your dog's overall health, so you should know the signs of oral disease and how you can prevent it.

TEETH DISEASES:

- Tartar build-up
- Tooth decay
- Gingivitis
- Infections
- Gum disease
- Bone loss

SYMPTOMS:

- Foul breath
- Visible deposits of tartar
- Discoloured teeth
- Fractured or missing teeth
- Sensitive teeth
- Refusal to eat

HOW TO CARE FOR YOUR PUPPY'S TEETH

- Brush teeth two to three times a week with a dog toothpaste or a canine toothbrush
- Use dental chews
- Use dental water
- Give your pooch chew toys designed to help clean tartar
- Check your dog's teeth regularly
- Ensure you feed your dog the correct diet

HOW TO BRUSH YOUR DOG'S TEETH

From an early age, you should desensitise your dog to brushing its teeth. You can reward your dog with treats if it doesn't pull away.

Lift your dog's cheek gently and brush its teeth from the front to the back, paying close attention to the gums.

DOG
GROOMING Sessions

Regular grooming sessions are necessary to prevent infections on your dog's skin. Grooming routines for dogs will differ depending on their breed and fur type. You should regularly check your dog's nails to prevent them from getting too long, as they can cause pain and difficulty walking.

NAIL CARE

When you have never cut a dog's nail before, the task might seem overwhelming. It is crucial that you know how short you can go since a dog can get anxious if an injury occurs during a trim. You can either use an automatic file or a manual cutter with a guide stopper. The general rule of thumb is to cut in small increments to avoid making mistakes that can cause injury to your dog.

The best time to cut your dog's nails is when the nails touch the floor, which normally takes around six to eight weeks. In order to determine whether the nails need to be cut, I slide a credit card under them. If I can't slide it with ease, then they need to be cut. Last, I prefer to file the edges so they are not sharp, and he won't scratch anyone.

FUR CARE

Dogs don't need to be bathed every day like humans; once a week is completely enough. However, I rinse with water, no shampoo, whenever my Labrador gets muddy or has had a swim in the river or the lake nearby.

Distinct type of coats require different care, and with some, you will have to learn how to trim the fur or use a groomer. With that said, they usually need trim about every six weeks. In between the groomer's visits, you can do the care on your own. The different coats include **smooth**, **double**, **long**, **heavy**, **silly**, **curly**, **wire**, and combination.

Brushing your dog's coat will keep it healthy and clean, and can be done at least two to three times a week, more often if your dog is in a shedding season You should brush your dog from the neck down to their tail, using firm strokes and bristle brush.

When you wash your dog, allow the hair to soak well first, before shampooing. You should shampoo twice and finish with the conditioner (only dog specific shampoo and conditioner). Then, blow dry the coat, brush it and trim if necessary.

WINTER
VERSUS SUMMER Care

When there are extreme weather conditions, you have to bear in mind that your dog might need special attention. Usually, dogs cope with temperatures between four degrees to twenty-three degrees. (Celsius). Smaller, short-coat breeds do not tolerate cold weather as much, whereas long-coat big dogs do not tolerate hot water. Either way, all dogs can get heatstroke or hypothermia if not looked at properly.

Summer

1. The danger of heatstroke is increased when temperatures reach over twenty-six degrees. Try walking your dog at the beginning or end of the day, to avoid the hottest part, and try not to overexert your dog.
2. You can take your dog swimming in streams, lakes, or dog-friendly beaches, or you can place a padding pool in the garden and let them splash around. Water is a great way to help cool your dog.
3. Ensure your dog stays hydrated, by providing fresh water at all times or giving ice lollies.
4. Make sure the pavement or street doesn't feel too hot to the touch with your hand. When it feels too hot for your hand, it is too hot for your dog's paws, which can burn them.
5. Do not leave your dog in the car, as the temperatures can rise quickly to dangerous levels.
6. If you want to help your dog regulate its temperature, you can use cooling mats or bandanas.
7. Dogs sweat in areas where they don't have fur, such as paws, ears, anus, and bellies. To help regulate their temperatures, dogs pant.

Winter

1. Cold weather, ice, snow and winter salt can cause sore, painful and cracked paws for your dog. To prevent this, after a walk clean your dog's paws and in between its toes. You might want to use a dog-specific lotion to help you keep your dog's paws moisturised.
2. Consider investing in boots for your dog, to protect their paws from the cold and ice.
3. Smaller breeds and short-coat breeds have a harder time keeping heat in the winter, so try to keep them warm by giving them a sweater or a coat.
4. Don't leave your dog unobserved for a long period in the cold, as they can get frostbite or hypothermia, even dogs with long and thick furs.
5. As it gets dark earlier, use reflective dog items to keep your dog visible to traffic and pedestrians.
6. Avoid letting your dog run over frozen lakes or rivers because they can break and fall through to ice.
7. Like us, dogs also love to curl up next to the heat source; however, ensure your dog does not go too close to radiators and fireplaces and burn itself.

LEARNING HOW TO CARE FOR YOUR PUP

WILL ENSURE YOU HAVE A LONG AND HAPPY LIFE WITH YOUR FUR FRIEND.

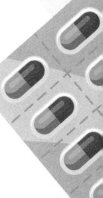

CHAPTER

SEVEN

FOOD
AND
Nutrition

DOG 101
FOOD

The quality of food and ingredients you give your dog has a direct impact on its overall health. While some dog owners may choose to feed their dog's commercial food, this can lead to digestive disorders, sensitivity issues and even problems like obesity, if they do not read the ingredients carefully.

In order to provide a healthy diet, you need to first learn about your dog's nutritional needs and which ingredients may compromise your dog's health. Depending on your dog's age, breed, activity level, medical condition and whether or not it has been de-sexed, the food requirements may vary, but the nutrients will remain the same.

Essential Nutrients

Carbohydrates

This nutrient is an important source of energy for your dog, as it provides glucose. Carbohydrates include sugars, starches, and fibre (which is comprised of complex carbohydrates). Food that includes carbohydrates are grains, fruit and vegetables.

Fibre

Although it falls under carbohydrates, we will talk about it separately, as it is considered a primary nutrient and not just an energy source. Fibre helps promote digestion and thus reduces the risk of digestive problems in dogs. There are two types of fibre, soluble and insoluble fibre. Soluble fibre dissolves in water, while insoluble fibre does not.

Soluble fibres are oat bran, psyllium husk, and apple pectin. Soluble fibres retain water, which helps to lower the risk of constipation.

Insoluble fibre includes wheat bran, corn bran, and cellulose. Insoluble fibre absorbs water, which helps to increase the bulk in the stool, which in turn helps to prevent constipation. It is important to know that dogs cannot derive a nutritional benefit from insoluble fibre.

Protein

This nutrient is used to build and repair muscles, as well as providing essential amino acids for making proteins. Proteins comprise amino acids, including taurine, arginine, lysine and methionine. Besides meats, we can find other sources of protein in eggs, milk and cheese.

Fat

Fat is used to create a barrier protecting other vital nutrients from being digested by enzymes in the gastrointestinal tract. It also assists in the absorption of essential fatty acids, which are essential in growth, helping to keep the coat healthy and shiny, and supplies energy (fat contains more calories than protein or carbohydrates). There are two types of fat: saturated and unsaturated.

Saturated fat is solid at room temperature and found in animal products, such as butter, eggs, and fatty meat.

Unsaturated fat is liquid at room temperature, and can be found in nuts, vegetable oils, certain fruits and vegetables, and fatty fish.

Vitamins

Vitamins are organic chemical compounds that help the body in many ways. They provide the raw materials for building proteins and the body's enzymes and help to regulate heartbeat, messages between the brain and nerves, nerve signals from the fingers to muscles, antibiotic resistance, hormone production and more.

Your dog should receive all the vitamins it needs through a well-balanced diet. If you have any doubts about your dog's intake, consult your vet or a certified pet nutritionist. Deficit and excess can both cause problems for your dog.

Minerals

Minerals are the most ubiquitous elements in the body. They are found in the blood, and in bones, teeth and other tissues. They are important for bone health, nerve conduction, muscle contraction and relaxation, blood clotting and many more essential functions.

As with vitamins, your dog should have all the minerals it needs through a well-balanced diet.

Water

Water is not usually consumed by dogs until they are extremely thirsty. If your dog isn't drinking enough water, add water to their food and give them fruits and vegetables that contain water, such as cucumbers and watermelon.

Dehydration in your dog can cause it to become weak, lose the ability to regulate its body temperature, have muscle cramps, and can even lead to heart problems. It is important to make sure that your dog has plenty of water available at all times.

How do I know if my dog's food is well balanced?

Whether you are feeding your dog wet, dry, raw or homemade food, you need to make sure that they are well-balanced in the ingredients included and provide an excellent source of all the nutrients, vitamins and minerals your dog needs.

Pet food brands are regulated in each country and should have an approval. For the US, it would be FDA and AAFCO, and for the UK, it would be the FSA and PFMA.

As part of the regulations, you should see the stamp of approval, the ingredient list, the nutritional value and feeding instructions.

How to read the labels properly?

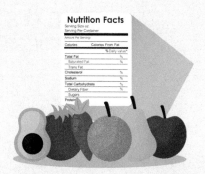

On the side of "Nutritional Facts" or "Guaranteed Analysis" is where you should find the levels of each nutrient in the food. The minimum that should be displayed is fats, protein, carbohydrates and fibre. The rest is voluntary and decided from the brand.

As a general rule of thumb, the higher the ingredient is on the list, the higher the presence of the ingredient in the food is, which should be written. Each ingredient needs to be specific. If it is ambiguous like "meats," I would recommend avoiding it as it can be a wide range of products with uncertainty of the quality.

How much does my dog need from each nutrient?

The daily amount of nutrients that a dog needs can differ from dog to dog, depending on age and activity levels. Puppies require more calories, calcium, protein and vitamins than adult dogs, and they also require more water. Therefore, the daily amount of nutrients that an adult dog needs is a little lower than for a puppy.

18-22%   5 -8%

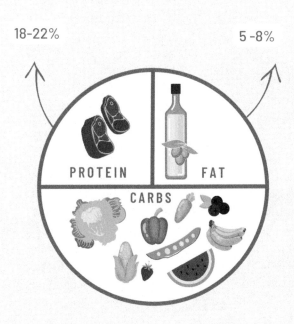

For puppies, according to AFFCO, the protein intake should be around twenty-two percent, and fat eight. For adult dogs, eighteen percent of protein, and five percent of fat. Note that, if your dog is a working dog, you need to consult with a certified nutritionist, as your dog's needs will greatly vary from a non-working adult dog.

Treats

Whether you are making your own treats or buying from the shop, again you should look at the ingredients list, even though it is not the main diet for you dog. Often, I buy dry meats and vegetables, rather than ready biscuits for my dogs.

FOODS **CAN Eat**
DOGS

There are plenty of foods that you can feed your dog at home that is safe, separate from its main meal. This said, do not replace your pooch's normal meals, or feed over ten percent additional calories from these options. If you want to create homemade dog meals, in the next chapter (page 122), I will share some recipes for treats. Before considering completely replacing your dog's regular food with homemade, you should consult with a certified pet nutritionist.

Fruits

Apples
Bananas✗
Blueberries
Cantaloupe
Coconut

Cranberries
Cucumber
Mango

Orange
Peach
Pears

Pineapple
Pumpkin
Raspberries
Strawberries
Watermelon

To prevent choking, remove peeling and seeds.

With corn, give only the seeds, without the cob.

Spinach
Sweetcorn

Celery
Green beans
Peas

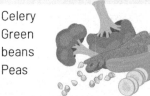

Vegetables
Broccoli
Brussels sprouts
Carrots

Meats
Beef Lamb Tilapia
Chicken Pork Turkey
Duck Salmon Venison

Cooked, with no spicing, and remove the bones.

Fibre
Plain pasta
Plain quinoa
Plain rice

Unsalted and remove the peeling

Nuts
Cashews
Peanuts

Honey

Cooked plain with no spices and sauces

Fish oil
Olive oil
Peanut butter

Fats
Cooked Eggs
Coconut oil

FOODS DOGS CAN'T Eat

The foods listed below have various levels of toxicity and can lead to poisoning in dogs or other long-term health issues. Everyone in your household should be educated on the items below, including children. You should not feed cooked food to dogs as often it will contain in various quantities some ingredients below.

Fruits

Cherries
Grapes
Raisins

Vegetables

Garlic
Mushrooms
Onion
Raw Potato
Tomato

Asparagus
Avocado
Corn on the cob

Meats

Bacon
Cooked Bones

Fat Trimmings
Ham

Spices

Nutmeg
Pepper
Paprika

Chilli
Cinnamon

Dough

Raw dough
Yeast dough

Caffeine

Soda
Tea

Coffee
Energy Drinks

Salty foods

Crisps
Pizza

Pretzels
Salted popcorn

Sugars

Gum
Sugar foods
Zylitol

Candy
Chocolate

Alcohol

Nuts

Cocoa
Macadamia

Raw Eggs

Marijuana

INGREDIENTS
IN DOGS' FOODS TO AVOID

With the ever-growing pet marketing, there is an overwhelming choice of dog food brands, which makes it harder for new owners who do not know how to choose the right one. There are some ingredients in dog food that can be bad for their health.

I've divided the ingredients into four groups; No nutritional value, Vague, Irritants and Health Damaging.

No nutritional value

The ingredients with no nutritional value are those that dogs don't need in their food but are commonly used. They can be highly harmful to the dog's health, and you should stay steer clear of them.

- Corn syrup
- Food colouring
- Propylene Glycol (PG)

Vague

As the ingredients are vague, it is impossible to guarantee the type of meat in the food. Because manufacturers can change the meats based on what is cheapest to purchase, you have no guarantee that you will receive the same quality next time you buy the same food from the same brand.

- Animal derivatives, digest or by-products
- Meat derivatives
- Meat meal
- Rendered fat

Irritants

Irritants are ingredients that can irritate your dog's stomach, intestines, skin, eyes or other organs and cause discomfort or illness to the dog.

- Carrageenan
- Monosodium Glutamate (MSG)
- Potassium Sorbate (PSG/E202)
- Potassium Sorbate (PSG/E202)
- Sodium Tripolyphosphate (STPP/E451)

Health Damaging

Health damaging ingredients are those that can cause long-term problems such as cancer, liver failure, heart failure, and more.

- Butylated Hydroxinolale (BHA/E320)
- Butylated Hydroxytoluene (BHT/E321)
- Melamine
- Monosodium Glutamate (MSG)
- Nitrates/nitrites
- Rawhide

COMMON FOOD Allergies

Just like humans, dogs can have allergies to certain foods. The disorder is called cutaneous adverse food reactions (CAFR), and you need a vet to properly diagnose if your pooch has one. However, if you notice any reactions after mealtime, it might not be a coincidence. Another thing to keep in mind is that your dog can develop a food allergy at any point in their life. It does not happen necessarily only at a young age. It can happen to senior dogs too.

Symptoms

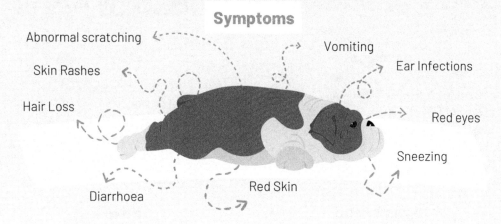

Abnormal scratching

Skin Rashes

Hair Loss

Diarrhoea

Red Skin

Vomiting

Ear Infections

Red eyes

Sneezing

How is it diagnosed?

If you notice any of the above-mentioned symptoms and suspect that your dog has a food allergy, it is imperative to consult a veterinarian. At the clinic, your vet will perform a test to confirm your dog does not have a skin infection or some sort of parasite manifestation. If your dog is cleared of this suspicion, your vet will request a food elimination diet for your pooch, that lasts eight to ten weeks. In the trial, you will get recommendations on how and which food you should feed your dog, and you must follow them strictly. I would recommend keeping a food diary and writing down your dog's reactions during this trial. Afterwards, you will talk to your veterinarian about the results and formulate an allergy treatment plan.

Common Allergens

- Beef
- Chicken
- Corn
- Dairy
- Eggs
- Lamb
- Soy
- Wheat

Treatment

There is no treatment for cutaneous adverse food reactions aside from avoidance. Your vet will recommend switching your dog to a hypoallergenic diet or a hydrolyzed protein diet. Sometimes, the clinic might prescribe antihistamines, corticosteroids or other drugs.

TYPES
OF DOG Food

If you have a healthy dog with no special needs, it is up to you and your budget which type of food you choose for your dog. The prices range between brands, and the quality and nutritional value largely depend on the ingredients, not the type of food.

Complete

For food to be considered a "Complete" dog food by AAFCO or PFMA, it must satisfy all the dog's nutritional requirements and, therefore, doesn't require supplements or other food.

Complementary

It is not designed to provide the full range of nutrients, but to be used as a topper or a mixer to the main meal.

Fresh Food

It's fairly new in the dog market food, and it's essentially based on the idea of a home-prepared complete food with human ingredients For the owner's convenience, it's sent on a subscription basis to be stored in the fridge and the freezer.

Before feeding, you need to defrost the food overnight. If unsealed, the food can be in the fridge for up to two weeks, sometimes less.

Raw

Raw food, as a concept, has been around for a while, and it still raises heated debates on its benefits. You can buy it frozen, complete or complementary, or some people make it themselves.

As with fresh food, you need to defrost overnight before feeding. However once defrosted, it can be in the fridge for a day or two, depending on the brand.

Wet

There are two types of wet food: complete and complimentary, and they comprise pâté or chunks in jelly or gravy. These types of foods are suitable for older dogs who struggle to chew, as they will break down in the stomach easier.

Once it's opened, feed it within twenty-four hours and keep it refrigerated.

Dry (Kibble)

Dry food is one of the most popular choices among dog owners because of its convenience. Besides being easy to store, it doesn't require much prep, and when you travel, you can easily take it along. There are five popular ways of preparing dry food:

Extrusion

The most popular process and the most processed once. The raw ingredients are dried and made into powders, which are mixed to create biscuit shapes and dried in hot air.

Baked

This is prepared at lower temperatures and slower to preserve more of the natural nutrients.

Freeze Dried

Multistep drying eliminates the need for preservatives and high processing by sucking moisture out of the food. The method is regarded as the most natural way of preparing kibble, but it also is the most expensive. Due to its lack of moisture, this kibble has to be soaked before serving to release its taste.

Cold Pressed

Before pressing into shapes, the raw ingredients are precooked, dried, and ground. Although the method is newer and less popular, it avoids the high temperatures of the extrusion process and retains more nutrients.

Air Dried

The raw mixture of nutrients is dried through heated air until all moisture is removed. It is considered closest kibble to a raw diet, as it preserves most of the nutrients, and it does not require fillers to bind the ingredients. Air drying gives a longer shelf life and does not require dehydration (depending on the brand).

How do you choose the right food?

The choice you make depends on a lot of factors: What is your budget? Do you have enough fridge space? Does your dog have special requirements? Is your dog a fussy eater?

With my dog, we went to almost every type of dog food until we opted for a mixture of dry and wet food. The dry food is slowly baked, and the wet food I use as a topper to change the tastes, and I like to add a sprinkle of dried vegetables and hydrate it. That was what works best for my dog, and he loves it, but it does not mean it will work for your dog.

Remember that whilst you are trying what works best for your dog, you need to change the food slowly to prevent gastrointestinal problems.

DOG MANNERS DURING Feeding Time

Dogs get excited about food, especially some breeds like Golden and Labrador retrievers. However, they need to learn to have manners. If you allow them to jump up before you give them their meal or when you are eating and then trying to steal your food, they have zero impulse control and probably no respect for you. To avoid this from happening, teach feeding time manners from day one.

If your dog jumps at you when you prepare its food, you must leave the food and ignore your pooch. There is no need for commands, even. After a few repetitions, your dog will learn what is expected.

Before you place down the food, ask your dog to "sit" and "wait" and only after its release command it can eat. However, if your dog rushes to its bowl before you have allowed it to, you must lift the bowl. Again, no need for any command if this happens. All you have to do is it repeat several times and your dog will figure it out.

When anyone from the household is eating, your dog must sit or stay down calmly. It takes a bit of time for your dog to learn this, especially if you are having long meals. However, you have to constantly reinforce it, and eventually, you will go calmly to a restaurant or a pub with your dog, knowing it won't jump and try to steal people's food.

You can either use a training mat or your dog's bed and use it to "settle" and give a few treats. It is best to start with smaller meals and shorter durations and, over time, increase it. You can positively reinforce and give treats when you are extending the time. In the end, once you finish your meal, you can give your dog praise and a treat for good behaviour.

A WELL-BALANCED DIET IS <u>VITAL</u> TO THE OVERALL HEALTH OF YOUR DOG.

CHAPTER

EIGHT

DOGGY
FOOD
Recipes

RECIPES FOR Kong

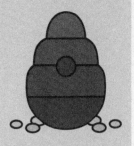

On page 113, I mention all the foods you can give to your dog, and you can choose and mix any of them in any way you like, plus add some dog food and treats. Here I will share some of my dog's favourite recipes.

Kong is a chew toy for dogs. It's made from durable rubber, and it's hollow on the inside with a hole. If your dog is bored and needs something to chew or play with, then Kong is a good choice!

On the market, you can find different Kong filters that you can use directly if you do not wish to make your own one.

Sprats Peanut Heaven

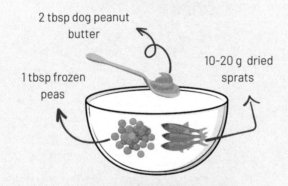

2 tbsp dog peanut butter

1 tbsp frozen peas

10-20 g dried sprats

Stuff the mixture into the Kong. You can adjust the amount of food depending on the size of the Kong you have.

Banana Sundae

Once you fill the Kong with the mixture, cover with cling film and freeze for three to four hours. Before serving to your dog, run under warm water for sixty seconds.

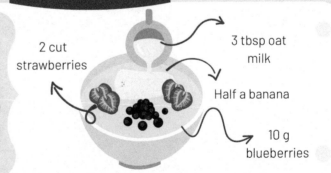

2 cut strawberries

3 tbsp oat milk

Half a banana

10 g blueberries

Ensure that when you fill the Kongs, you leave an air passage from the top and the bottom hole to avoid potential suction accidents.

Meat Feast

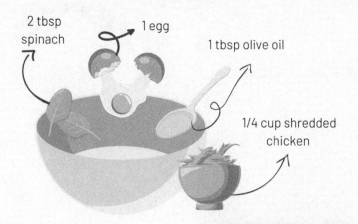

1/4 cup shredded carrots

2 tbsp mash sweet potato

1/4 cup water

1/4 cup cooked salmon

Mix all the ingredients, and you can serve fresh or frozen.

1/4 cup chicken pâté

1/4 cup cooked turkey

2 tbsp spinach

1 egg

1 tbsp olive oil

1/4 cup shredded chicken

Sunday Breakfast

Mix and cook the ingredients in a pan. You can serve frozen or fresh. If you serve fresh, wait until the temperature drops to room temperature.

Lazy Dinner

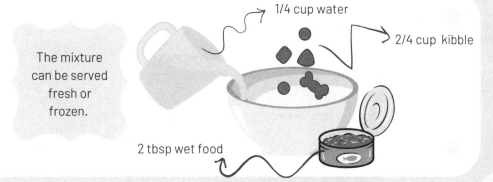

1/4 cup water

2/4 cup kibble

The mixture can be served fresh or frozen.

2 tbsp wet food

RECIPES
FOR Lick-mats

Made from durable silicone, lick-mats are a great enrichment activity you can easily prepare at home. Licking reduces stress and anxiety in dogs, promotes oral health, and makes them work for their food.

Minced Meat

Pureed Vegetables

Mashed Fruits

You can serve fresh or frozen.

Dog Peanut Butter

Honey

Thinned Pumpkin

Plain Yogurt

Similarly, as with Kong, you can experiment with the ingredients, as long it's food that it's not toxic. You can spread a single ingredient, or you can mix a few – your choice!

Supervise your dog while it's eating so that it is not chewing on the mat, as it can be a potential choking hazard.

RECIPES
FOR
Ice Lollies

An ice lolly is a great summer treat for your dog. Besides cooling your dog down, ice lollies, like lick-mats, can reduce stress and keep them entertained. You can prepare ice lollies by shaping and freezing them yourself using a muffin tray, or you can easily buy already frozen from a pet shop.

Once they are frozen, you just have to give them to your dog and let it lick the ice.

Do not give your dog popsicles made for humans, as they will be full of toxic ingredients for your dog.

Chicken Soup

1 cup chicken broth

1/4 cup chopped carrots

2/4 cup chicken pieces

Summer Paradise

Blend the ingredients together and freeze.

2/3 cup watermelon (remove seeds)

1 banana

1/3 cup plain yogurt

Peanut Butter Ice Creams

1/4 whole peanuts

2/4 cup dog peanut butter

1 tsp honey

1/4 cup plain yogurt

RECIPES FOR Biscuits

With all honesty, from all the recipes I've shared, biscuits is perhaps the one that requires the most time and involvement. Do you have to do it? No. Is it fun? Yes. Your dog will love to get involved with baking it, and you know that you have made clean, nutritious and delicious biscuits for your pup.

Banana and Peanut Butter

2 eggs

Mix the ingredients, and add water if necessary until it becomes a smooth dough.

1 cup dog peanut butter

1/4 cup water

1 banana

1 cup of the whole wheat flour

1 tsp honey

Once the dough is smooth, roll it out to a thickness of one to two centimetres. Use whichever biscuit cutter you like to cut it. For all recipes, at 170°C for fifteen minutes.

Serve at a room temperature.

Sunday Roast

You can boil the sweet potato and chicken together and use the broth for an Ice lolly.

Mix the ingredients and make them into small balls, or bake in a silicone mould.

1 tbsp chopped parsley

1/4 cup tinned peas

1 egg

1/4 cup mash sweet potato

2/4 cup finely chopped boiled chicken

Blueberry Oats

Process the oats in a food blender until you have a fine powder. Then mix all the ingredients until you get a smooth mixture. Form into small balls, and press with a fork. Proceed to bake.

5 cups rolled oats

2 eggs

2 cups blueberries

1/4 cup yoghurt

Pumpkin Cake

Mix the ingredients into a smooth dough. Roll it out, cut into shapes and bake until hardened.

2 cups canned pumpkin

3 tbsp oat milk

1 egg

1 cup whole wheat flour

1/2 tsp cinnamon

3 tbsp soften coconut oil

Fish Fingers

Mix the ingredients in a bowl adding water if necessary to get a smooth consistency. Put the dough between two sheets of baking paper and roll out, then cut into shapes. Bake until hardened.

1/2 cup steamed shredded salmon

3 eggs

1/2 cup steamed shredded cod

3 tbps whole wheat flour

2 tbsp soften coconut oil

CHAPTER

NINE

SOCIALISING AND Training

BE YOUR DOG'S Leader

Before we even proceed with dog training in socialisation, understand the importance of you being a leader in your dog's eyes. When we talk about you being your dog's leader, we are not talking in the sense of a pack leader, although there are some training methods that are based on pack leader theory and hierarchy. Instead, what I am meaning is a human (you) leading your dog in the right direction, and building trust in the relationship.

Why do you need to be your dog's leader?

Throughout the lifetime of your dog, there will be many situations where your dog can become distracted, confused, stressed and scared. In these situations, your dog will want to go back to you for reassurance and guidance, but if you are not their leader, your dog would probably choose to run from you. In any of the mentioned situations, a leadership role is very important. That said, for your dog to turn to you for guidance, you have to work on your relationship as a leader from the beginning, as it won't just happen on its own.

How to be your dog's leader?

The qualities you need to possess to be a leader in your dog's eyes aren't much different from being a leader in within your peers. Be kind, clear, consistent, calm, and assertive. Dogs need to earn and work for their privileges. Giving them freedom too early will only teach your dog that you are not a capable leader. If this happens, your dog will lose respect for you and will start making decisions on its own, rather than looking up to you.

Yes, we get our dogs to be a loving part of the family, but to be good and responsible owners, we need to understand dogs' mentality. When we understand it, we will handle our pooches better.

Dogs like to be busy and feel like they have a job or something to do. When you train your dog, you help them be occupied mentally, and they are happy as they get to prove themselves and please you. Dogs are very smart creatures and they can learn a lot from you. So use it. Show them how and what you want from them. If they get it right, reward them. If they get it wrong, correct them.

Be Kind

If your dog makes a mistake, or there has been an accident, you should be kind, redirect and show what you want your pup to do. Punishing and yelling will make your dog fear you, and it will not want to listen to you. And sometimes, punishing also makes your dog angry, and it will want to fight with you because it is scared. Kindness will go a long way. You want your dog to love you and want to come to you and please you, not fear you.

01

Be Clear

02

If your dog doesn't understand what you ask from it, if you say too many commands, or if you say something in a tone that the dog doesn't recognise as a command, your dog won't know what to do and will make mistakes. Be clear and specific. Use short commands that the pup can understand.

Be Calm

Dogs learn and respond best when they are calm and concentrated. If you are not calm, the dog will not listen to you.

If you panic or get angry when your dog runs away from you or in another stressful situation, your dog will feel it and would ignore your commands because of the tone of your voice.

04

Be Consistent

03

If the commands change, or the rules change, the dog will get confused. So keep it consistent and your dog will not have much trouble understanding and following your lead.

05

Be Assertive

Your dog needs to know that you are in charge and that you make the rules. They need to understand that you are their leader, so they treat you like one. That doesn't mean you shout or punish them, but it means that when you give a command, it has to happen.

For example, if you ask your dog to sit, and it doesn't, push its bottom down. Do it firmly, but don't hurt your dog. Your body and your voice need to be strong so that your dog knows you are an influential person.

Your pooch will respect you only if you look in control, and they know they can trust you and always come to you when they want something to happen, no matter what.

DOG 101
TRAINING

With training, you are creating a trusting relationship with your dog. However, training, when done improperly, could harm the relationship between you and your puppy. So training needs to be done clearly so that your furry friend understands what we expect of it.

To avoid confusing your dog, the first step is to learn the basic training vocabulary and use the same word for the commands. Don't use different words for the action.

The second step to having a great relationship with your puppy is making sure you set clear boundaries for it. For example, if you don't want behaviours – such as no pets on the couch or bed, never jump over anything etc – make these rules are consistent at all times so it knows what is expected. Make sure it stays within those boundaries, or else there will be trouble and it won't listen.

Third, when training your dog, you are also training yourself as well. With that being said, trust between you and your dog should increase with time, so learning how to properly show love for your pup is important.

Training allows you to communicate with your dog using clear signals so that it can understand what is expected of it.

BASIC COMMANDS
THAT YOUR PUP SHOULD Master

Training your pup is a great way to build an excellent relationship with it. It loves pleasing you and being mentally stimulated while it's learning new commands, which also makes it fun for both of you! From page 153, we'll go over the basics commands and how to teach them.

Training your dog requires patience and a lot of repetition. However, you only need to dedicate five to fifteen minutes per session for training! Most dogs can learn up 160 different words so choose wisely what commands you plan for them.

Yes

Their Name

No

Come

Leave it

Get it

Drop it

Wait

In

Enough

Ok

Sit

Stand

Settle

Bring it

Off

This way

Touch

Watch

Go for a walk?

Good dog/boy/girl

Are you hungry?

Outside

Bed

Paw

Down

Stay

Heel

With me

DIFFERENT
METHODS OF DOG
Training

There are many different methods of dog training and a lot of debates about what is right and wrong, what works and what doesn't. I will introduce you to the most popular ones, but keep in mind have in mind that in this book all the training is based on "Positive Reinforcement." This is the method that has worked best with my dogs, and I have even trained my cats with it. I am not kidding.

You can, of course, use any training method. However, remember that you have to stay consistent. If you keep changing the way you train your pup, it will only lead to confusion and low to no progress. My advice is to do your reading and research before you commit to any method.

1. Positive Reinforcement

It's based on rewarding the dog when it is doing what you want it to do and failing to reward if it is not. It is one of the most popular training methods because it builds an emotional bond between owner and dog. Essentially, you are conditioning your dog to understand which are the good behaviours.

By not punishing your dog to discourage it from doing something (negative reinforcement/positive punishment), you are building confidence in your dog and improving your relationship with It. Positive reinforcement works, and it's backed by a growing amount of scientific research.

2. Negative Reinforcement

As briefly mentioned above, this method is based on punishing the dog every time they do something bad.

This is also a very popular method. Unfortunately, it doesn't work well with how the dog's mind is structured and learning works. The main problem with using this method is that we are punishing our dogs to discourage them from doing something, but they don't understand why they are being punished, which brings their confidence down, breaks your relationship as they start to fear you and slows their progress. The end will result is that your dog will start avoiding you instead of being excited to spend time with you and do more training.

3. Alpha Dog or Dominance

This method was based on the belief that humans are the "pack leaders," and the dogs follow and obey and submit to your will, so the owner needs to be dominant.

This method dates back hundreds of years, and it's still used today in many ways, including dog training. In this method, is believed that if you let your dog take over, it will be more aggressive or just not obedient and listen to you. Essentially, if you use this method, you won't be raising a companion, but more a dog that will be afraid of you. It will come to you only when called, and out of fear, not out of love.

4. Clicker Training

The popularity of his method has been growing for the last few years, and it's based on teaching the dog by using a clicker. It is used to communicate with the dog in a quick and precise way without you having to say anything or do anything. The clicker is used as an attention grabber to let the dog know they are doing something correctly, reward-based training. The clicker is used to mark the exact moment of the desired behaviour.

DIFFERENT TYPE
OF DOG TRAINING Equipment

In the past, trainers have had to work with limited tools to get their pooch to behave. Thankfully, we now have an array of dog training equipment that can help you shape and mould your pup. But before you rush out and buy everything on the market, it's important to know what gear you need and what gear is just a waste of money.

Essentials

Crate

Some people dislike to crate train, but I believe it's the best way to teach house rules and potty training. However, remember it is not a punishment tool or nor should you leave your dog there for long periods (besides sleep time or travel).

Colar

Your dog should be comfortable wearing a collar, as if it's not, it will be harder to leash train it. Your dog should also wear ID tags with your contact information. This is essential in case your dog gets lost.

Normal lead

This most popular training tool is used for walking, obedience and other basic tricks. The standard length it's four feet, and your dog should learn to know that length if you want your pooch to walk nicely next to you on the lead.

Retractable or Long Lead

With it, you give your dog a false sense of freedom, whilst you still have control. It's useful for teaching your dog a strong recall. However, it should not be used for everyday walks. Your dog should understand that it is different equipment and that only this lead allows free time, else you can confuse your dog as it won't understand why the lead length changes.

For Pullers

Head Harness

A device that rests loosely over a dog's nose and neck and prevents the dog the pulling. It redirects your pooch by turning its head when they pull ahead of you.

Halters are not muzzles and should not be mistaken for such. In a head harness, your dog can still freely open its mouth and enjoy treats. They are a very effective training tool, and your dog will become more focused when it works with this equipment.

No Pull – Harness

These work similarly to head harnesses, as they will turn your dog to the side when they pull ahead. They are similar as to a normal harness. The biggest difference is that they have a loop at the front where you clip the lead and it's essentially what makes it a no-pull harness.

A traditional harness would not start the pulling or encourage it. However, it will make it easier to control your dog and put less pressure on your dog when they pull. I would not recommend you to use a normal harness if your dog already pulls on the lead.

Dog training equipment for strong pulling dogs should be used as a temporary measure whilst you are training your dog, not as a solution. For example, it can be used when you are in a rush and you know you can't focus on training your dog on this walk; or when another person walks your dog and you do not want to ruin all the training that you have done up to this point.

When I worked with a trainer, we were recommended to use a halti. At first, I was hesitant, as I thought it my hurt my dog. However, pretty quickly I realised that this equipment does not hurt or harm your pet in any way.

We ended up using the halti with my Labrador, as he was getting stronger than me, and when he pulled, I was struggling to hold him. (Not my proudest moment.) However, I had to use it for a month as he pretty quickly understood that by pulling, he wouldn't reach his destination any faster.

Muzzle

It is very useful dog equipment in the prevention of biting or eating dangerous things for your pup, but you must gently train your dog into it. Also, the best prevention is good obedience training. So if you must use a muzzle, try to train them, so they do not need it.

Clicker

It is useful when you train your dog as it will associate the click with good behaviour. However, it makes you and your dog training reliant on it.

Whistle

It is an excellent tool to get your pet's attention, but in order to get used to them, your dog needs to associate it with something positive and be trained to do so. Plus, not all dogs like the sound of it.

Training Mat

Similarly to the clicker and the whistle, it can be useful, especially when you want to teach your dog to settle. However, it risks making your dog reliant on it, and then you will have to teach your pup again if you remove the mat or you don't have it.

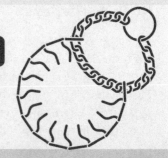

Prong or Choke Collar

It's not good for training, and it can hurt your dog and damage your relationship by creating fear. It is used to stop pulling in the negative reinforcement method of training.

Shock or E-Collar

It's an alternative choke collar and used not only to stop pulling but other unwanted behaviour. The trainer will press a button that will send shock waves to the dog. It can be extremely damaging for your dog's physical and mental health.

No equipment will train your dog into obedience. It will be your direction, guidance and consistency that will achieve the results.

DOG
SOCIALISTING 101

If you have a new dog or even just a new puppy, one of the first things that every owner should learn is how to socialise their pet to feel confident and comfortable in every environment.

Avoid overwhelming your dog.

Exposing your dog to too many new people or other dogs at once can make them more stressed. Instead, introduce them to new places, experiences, people or dogs one at a time.

Start young, if possible

The best time to socialise with your dog is when its young. If you are already aware of the personality trait of your dog and an altercation occurred, it's best to talk to a vet or professional dog trainer. Some dogs will naturally be more skittish than others when meeting other people or dogs or going to unknown places.

Do not say "good boy/girl" when it's scared.

This will only reinforce its fear and make them fearful of you. Instead, check on them regularly and try to make eye contact with them so they know you are there.

Dog socialising is an essential part of every dog's life and will help them grow into well-rounded, confident dogs. Being the owner of a well-socialised dog can give you peace of mind on your walk, when having guests, during travel or visits to the veterinarian. In the next few pages, we will discuss the topic in more depth.

PUPPY
DESENSITISATION List

Dog desensitisation does not stop with just "socialising your dog". In fact, well-socialised dogs need to be desensitised to each and every single thing that can frighten or startle them. Socialisation continues beyond puppyhood and into adolescence and adulthood.

Start slow, and introduce them to new things gradually and make it like a game. Your dog will find it easier and will remember it as a positive and fun experience. Don't forget to award positive reactions and behaviour with praise and treats.

Dogs

Children

Parks

Hoover

Cats

Groomer

Beaches

Women

Men

Cars

Rivers

Bicycle

Noises

Swimming

Pet stores

Construction sites

People with accessories

Veterinary clinics

Different surfaces

Car parks

DESENSETASING

& SOCIALISING
Rules

As you introduce your pup to new situations, people and environments, track their progress. Pay attention to their behaviour, notice any warning signs, and interfere if any situation might cause a stressful event.

1 Children

Desensitisation is most effective with children. They can be trained to approach the dog and pet it or play with toys in the yard. Never leave children and puppies unsupervised.

2 Other pets at home

If you have another pet, introduce it gradually and supervise closely. If you have a cat, teach your dog not to bite it.

3 Trains, buses, cars, planes

Desensitise your dog to all of these situations. If it gets used to them, it will no longer be nervous .

4 Friends and family

Dogs can't resist petting and playing and can get overexcited when they get a lot of attention. Causing jumping up, running and biting. Control your dogs with a lead and positive reinforcement.

5 Neighbours and strangers

Go for a walk where you might meet and greet neighbours and strangers, and train them to stay close to you in a sitting and calm position.

6 Other dogs

Your dog needs to know basic commands before they can play – sit, heel, no, come, leave it. You should keep them on the lead initially and reward good behaviour, pulling back when they react negatively.

IT'S CRUCIAL
IN PREVENTING
BEHAVIOUR
Issues

7 Grooming

Grooming is a really important to get your dog used to. Make it fun and give the dog treats throughout the process.

8 Noise

Loud noises can frighten dogs, so teach them how to cope with them. Fireworks, storms and alarms are common things dogs are scared off and may react badly to. Start by playing them on your phone at a low volume and gradually increase.

9 Dog parks and crowds

Dog parks and crowds are places that your dog may be shy or overly excitable. Start by walking in one where you know the dogs there and slowly progress to larger parks. Reward good behaviour.

10 Enclosed spaces

Enclosed spaces can make a dog timid. Start by games and treats in their crate, car boot, etc.

11 Alone time

Sometimes a dog may be too anxious to be left alone and will need extra care. To avoid separation anxiety, slowly introduce the idea of leaving them alone. Start with ten minutes and slowly increase.

12 Deal with issues immediately

If your dog is overstimulated or frightened, deal with the problem immediately. You don't need to wait for it to occur. Their body language can be quite telling. It is crucial to prevent behaviour issues.

Dogs can be just like people. And they can overcome being shy and scared if they're taught how to be more confident.

COMMON MISTAKES
WHEN SOCIALISING
YOUR DOG

Socialisation for your dog it is indeed crucial to their wellbeing, but how do you go about doing it? As a dog owner, you should know that your dog's socialising begins when they are just a few weeks old and continues to the day they die. But is there really any certain way to successfully socialise your dog? Well, with socialising fur children, the answer is yes! There are some mistakes that many first-time pet owners make when trying to socialise their dogs and these mistakes could cause more than one kind of harm to your pup.

Socialising your dog too much

This is just as bad as not socialising them enough. Dogs dislike to be in a state of confusion, so give them enough time to get used to any situation that is presented. It is suggested for the first couple of months your dog be introduced to new environments at least once a week.

Overwhelming your dog

A day out with your dog around town can be fun; however, do not attempt it with a young pup. When you are starting socialisation, start small, and don't plan a big day out in busy places, if your dog hasn't had been exposed to similar environments. Introduce new environments gradually, and observe how your pup reacts, as the last thing you want is for your dog to get overwhelmed, stressed and anxious.

Not turning a negative experience into a positive

This is the fundamental mistake that many owners make when faced with a difficult situation. If your dog gets scared by a train noise, counteract it. Call their name, distract them with a toy or a treat, so they do not associate train noises with something scary, but they remember a positive experience.

Coddling your dog

Do not, under any circumstance, make the mistake of turning a negative experience into a positive one, as an excuse to coddle your dog. If your dog is displaying signs of aggression or anxiety, do not encourage it by saying "it's okay", "good boy", petting them or lifting them up. If you do that, you are not only rewarding this behaviour, you are not building their confidence, and you are encouraging it to repeat the behaviour the next time your dog finds itself in a similar situation. Your dog is looking up to you as a leader, so be one and recognise the signs, avoid the situation and redirect your dog with a command or away from the situation.

Letting everyone pet your dog

No one likes strangers entering their personal space. So why would you allow this to be done to your dog? Next time someone comes and tries to pet your dog because "it's so cute," stop it. See how your dog feels around this person. If your dog hides behind you, do not let them pet your dog. Especially for people who go and shove their hand in front of your dog's face or on try to pet it from above. This can be is a major cause of fear and anxiety in many dogs. Instead, you can give the other person a treat and ask them to lower themselves to the dog level and offer the treat. Let your dog choose if it wants to go near them by itself.

Forcing your dog to say "Hi" to every dog

06

It's quite a common mistake which can lead to having a reactive dog. Your pooch can be turned reactive towards other dogs for two reasons. One is because it had terrible experiences and it's anxious. Two is because pooch thinks all dogs are friendly and expects to say hi and to play with every dog, and associates other dogs with more fun than you. Dogs don't need dog friends to be happy. Your family is their pack; other dogs are from other packs. Therefore, they can be friendly. It is actually good to be friendly, but they don't have to be friends. Ensure that you stay as a leader on your walks, and your dog is happy to stay with you.

Commands need to be taught in the right context and in the right time to achieve the desired results.

WHY YOU SHOULD
AVOID DOG
PARKS?

At first glance, it seems like taking your dog places and letting him play with other dogs might be an easy way to make him happy. And while that is partly true, there are a lot more disadvantages than advantages in these unregulated open spaces.

Dog size

In these parks, often there aren't designated areas for different size dogs, which can often lead to accidents.

Every dog can become aggressive

Even the friendliest dogs can react aggressively in a flight or fight situation if they feel threatened. This can be very dangerous, especially if they are not under control.

You don't know the other dogs

It's a mistake to assume that every dog has friendly or obedient, or that the dog owner would see understand their dog and the others dog's body language. In fact, most people can't read their dog's body language, which can lead to accidents.

Contracting different diseases

As no one at the park is checking if all dogs have had their treatments and vaccinations, you have no guarantee that all dogs are not carrying parasites. Dogs that play together often have a high success rate of picking up diseases from one another –worms, ticks, fleas, kennel cough, giardia, and the list goes on.

Risk of injury or even death

It is not uncommon for things to get out of hand quickly. More often smaller and friendlier dogs are at a higher risk of being injured if a dog game turns into a fight, and the bigger dog ends up hurting or killing the smaller or weaker one.

HOW TO CRATE Train

Crate training is one of the most common methods of house training. Dogs naturally use a den to sleep, so if you have a crate where they can safely rest, you'll have better success with potty training and destructive behaviour.

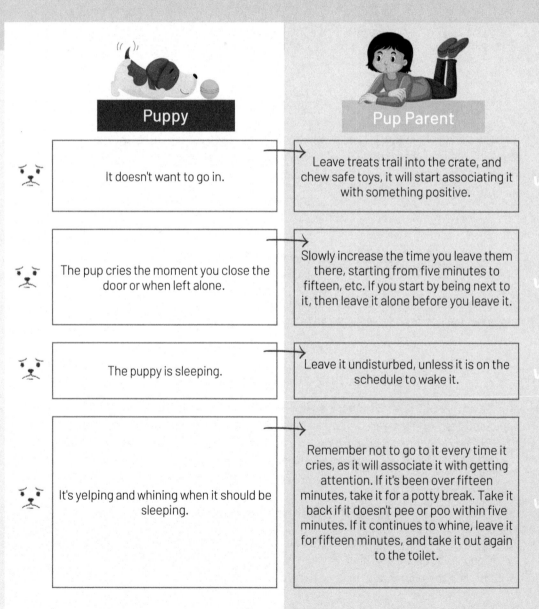

Puppy	Pup Parent	
It doesn't want to go in.	Leave treats trail into the crate, and chew safe toys, it will start associating it with something positive.	✓
The pup cries the moment you close the door or when left alone.	Slowly increase the time you leave them there, starting from five minutes to fifteen, etc. If you start by being next to it, then leave it alone before you leave it.	✓
The puppy is sleeping.	Leave it undisturbed, unless it is on the schedule to wake it.	✓
It's yelping and whining when it should be sleeping.	Remember not to go to it every time it cries, as it will associate it with getting attention. If it's been over fifteen minutes, take it for a potty break. Take it back if it doesn't pee or poo within five minutes. If it continues to whine, leave it for fifteen minutes, and take it out again to the toilet.	✓

As much as you are training your dog, train yourself and other household members to resist the urge to cuddle the crying puppy or disturb it just because it's so cute when it's sleeping.

Puppy	Pup Parent
The pup peed inside the crate.	You left it in the crate for too long. Decrease the time next time.
Your puppy is resentful towards the crate.	Ensure that your dog does not associate the crate with punishment. Many owners use a crate for time-outs, or to keep the dog out of harm's way if you have other pets or small children and the dog needs to be separated from them temporarily. If this is what you're doing, make sure you get it there positively and don't ignore your dog once it has been placed there.
Your dog is protective and territorial towards its crate	It might feel threatened or does not see you as the pack leader. If this is the case, let it come to you, and be gradual with your interactions. If you are not authoritative enough, you should have a series of rules with the crate and enforce them immediately, perhaps even moving it.

HOW TO POTTY Train?

Puppies thrive on a regular schedule. By following the schedule, they learn when it's time to eat, when to play, and when to go to the bathroom. Puppy bladder control typically lasts one hour for every month of age. If your puppy is two months old, it can hold its wee for about two hours. Make sure they don't go longer than this between bathroom breaks or they will have an accident.

Naptime must be included in the schedule, and it must not be disturbed. Take your pooch outside in the designated area for its bathroom break first. If the pup does not do so, put it for around twenty minutes in its crate and repeat. Let it nap only after it has relieved itself. Let it sleep for approximately two hours. After nap time is over, take your pup for a wee in the same designated area.

Observe the pup behaviour, as it often shows when it needs to go by circling around or barking next to the door.

Create a schedule
The schedule has to work for you, and have in mind your puppy needs: sleep, food, walk, bathroom and playtime.

Stick to it
Be strict with yourself and the rest of the family. Every change you make will confuse the pup and lead to accidents.

Ignore accidents
Do not yell or punish your dog for any accidents. It can damage your relationship. The pup does not know it did something wrong.

Reward good behaviour
Reward your pup with a treat and praise for going when and where they should. The more you do it, the better choices it will make.

As they age, you can increase the interval between bathroom breaks. A change in the schedule calls for you to be present and attentive, in order to prevent an accident.
On page 203, you can find an example of a puppy schedule.

You shouldn't treat training your dog like a **JOB** but as an opportunity to

BOND

with your new best friend.

HOW TO TRAIN
THE BASIC
Commands

The best way to approach teaching a puppy is pretty similar to how you would teach a toddler – through a game and with lots of praise for good behaviour. The biggest difference is that you can't explain to your dog with words what you want them to, so you have to lure them with a treat into the position you want them to be in.

To begin, it is best to choose a place with no distraction and keep them on their lead. As they progress, you can add distraction and give them freedom to make it more challenging for them.

Note:
Be patient and consistent, and keep the training sessions short. Remember, you want them to succeed every time, and you want them to learn to make good choices on their own. The best way to do this is not to let them fail, by giving too much freedom too early.

Training Schedule:
You can vary the times during the day at which you teach your puppy. It is not advisable to have over three training sessions per day, especially at the beginning.

1   Its name

The first ever command that you should teach from the very first day. It should not take them over one to three days, but you must continue training their name beyond that time.

Start by letting them get distracted, then call its name enthusiastically and luring them to you with a treat. Once it comes to you say "Yes" give it the treat and praise it. Repeat a few times.

Note:
If your puppy's attention is fading, finish the session with a praise and playtime.

2 Yes

The "yes " command is a positive reinforcement command that has to be associated always with a praise, a treat or a game. (Dogs have different motivators - more on page 85) It is a sign for your dog to know that what it's doing is right. A clicker word to mark the exact moment of the correct behaviour.

Note:
It's important to use the command in a timely manner – not before or after the action, but right when the action is happening.

The way to teach it is to say "Yes" during an action you want them to perform and follow it up with a reward. Like when your dog is sitting, the moment their bottom touches the ground you say "Yes" and follow up with a reward.

No 3

The command is only used to mark the precise moment, when your dog is doing something they should not with the goal to interrupt it,

The way to teach it is to say "No" firmly with a clear, loud voice and to interrupt the action. Follow up with redirecting the behaviour and saying "yes" when the pup does the right thing. This way, your pooch would know what to do instead, because it has been encouraged it to do it.

Note:
Do not scorn your dog, when, or after you say "No." You want to interrupt the behaviour only with this command.

Let's say you pup bites you. The moment you pup does it, you say "No." You stop the game and the biting and redirect it by giving it a toy that it can bite instead. Praise the correct behaviour by saying "yes" .

Okay 4

The release command usually helps your dog to know what is coming but to wait calmly until it's allowed. It's used to release them from a "stay" command.

Occasions where you use it are: before greetings, before entering through any door, before food, before running off the leash and more.

Start your dog in a sit position. After it has stayed for a few moments in it say "Okay" and throw a treat, so the dog has to break its position. After a few successful tries, say "Okay" without moving and luring them with a treat. Praise with "Yes" and reward the correct behaviour.

Note:
Do not reward breaking off a command unless you have said the word.

Over time, you can raise the challenge and use words with similar sounds to test your dog's focus. Do it in different environments and add different distractions until it masters it.

5 Drop it

"Drop it" is a command that can again be lifesaving. Dogs have the tendency to chew on things that can be harmful to it. Start by luring your pup with a high reward treat to drop its toy, and reward it with a "Yes" and a treat. If the dog is not food motivated, you can do it for a swap with another exciting toy.

Note:
Wait for your pup to drop the item before you reward it.

Your dog needs to associate "drop it" with getting something, else it might choose to hold on to what that it finds exciting, but is bad for it - like a sock, battery or chocolate.

6 Off

Naturally dogs jump up, as they want to be near you. Although as a pup, you might find it cute, it is not nice when it gets its muddy paws on you or a stranger.

Next time you find your dog jumping on you, the couch or any other area it is not supposed to be on, lure them down with a treat, and say the command. Once the pup is on all fours, praise it and give a treat.

This command can be only taught in moments when your dog is misbehaving, so you need to keep treats near, until they learn it.

Be patient. It might take a couple of months before they stop doing it, so you have to stay consistent.

Note:
Do not allow for your pup to jump up on you, or furniture sometimes and other times tell them to get off. Be consistent, or your pup will not understand why it allowed sometimes or not others.

Come 7

It's an extremely important command that can sometimes save your pup's life. The command should be so ingrained that your pup shows up even if other people are calling it, it's playing with other dogs, or there are any other exciting distractions. Your pup should become proficient that it does not need a lure to come to you.

Get your dog to sit, then say "come" and lure it to you. Repeat it a few times, praise and reward each time it comes to you. After it has learned what "come" means, the next step is to lure it in and say "come" when it's at some distance from you. Each time your pup masters the environment and the challenge, bring it up a notch and introduce minor distractions. If it fails, go back to the previous level, do not repeat the mistake.

Note:
Make sure you set your pup up for success. It is essential it associates "come" with coming to you, instead of when it wants to.

Sit 8

A foundation command, that is a base for more complex ones. Depending on how excitable your pup is, you might not teach it in the first session. Do not worry if that is the case. In the second or maybe third, they will understand.

Start by having your dog in a neutral standing position. Hold a treat in your hand and bring it to its nose. Naturally, it will lift its head to get it, use that moment and move it into an arc until you bring the pup to a sitting position. Praise it by saying "Yes" and giving the treat.

Note:
Do not allow and praise jumping up for the treat.

9 Down

Dogs can get very excited in new environment or around new people, having to be able to get them into "down" position will help with that excitement and calm them.

To teach you pup, you will start from a "sit" position and lure it with a treat with palm facing down. Drag your palm to the floor with the treat. Once they lay down, say "yes" and reward them after.

Note:
It's easier to teach them to lie down when they are tired, as opposed to in the morning when they are excitable.

Give the treat only after they are laying down, not before, or if they moved from it.

Next step would be to say "Down" without luring them to the position. After this is mastered at home, you can add up different environments and challenges.

10 Wait

It is one of the most-used commands you will have, as you will teach your dog patience by asking it to wait for different things.

Start by putting your dog in front of something it wants – pass by the door, it's dinner or a treat. Put your hand in the air and say "wait." When it does, you can say "Okay" and let them have whatever they were waiting for as a reward.

You can up the challenge by moving away from your dog, running, leaving the room and expecting it to "wait" until you call it.

Your dog does not need to be next to you to for you to say "wait" or to release it with "okay", "come" or another command that it is waiting for.

Note:
"Wait" command differs from a "stay" command because your dog is expecting what it will do next. It's waiting for work. Whereas in stay, it has is to stay until you come next to release it.

Stay 11

Another basic and lifesaving command. It can stop a dog from running into the street, going to a dog that can be dangerous and more.

Start in a quiet place by asking your dog to sit or down. Then, give it a signal with your hand (like stop sign). Once your dog is in the desired position, move. Do the hand gesture and say "Stay." If you dog moves, say "No." Repeat until it doesn't. It's important as soon as it gets it right for you to praise and give the treat, so it knows for what it is being praised for. This command needs to be trained consistently, in different locations, with different distractions.

Note:
If you do the command with the hand gesture, over time you can just use the gesture and your dog will stay.

Do not let your dog move out of "stay" command until you release it with a double pat on the shoulder and "okay". In this command, your dog must stay in position a pat on the shoulder (release command) no matter what.

12 Stand

This command is when you want to get your dog to get up from a sitting position to a standing position.

When your dog is in a "sit" position, take a treat and move it from the nose to under the chin. That should cause your dog to stand to get the treat.

In some situations, the dog might be too clumsy or excitable and not get the command, then you would like to put the treat in a small cup or bowl and perform the same movement.

Say the word "Stand" and reward with the treat only after your dog has done the command successfully.

Note:
As much as it is a simple command to teach, it's quite easy as well to be rewarded when your pup did not execute the command properly, so be patient and observant when you reward.

Touch 13

It is a simple command that you can teach your pup when you are just starting out with dog obedience training. Why? It's great a great foundation, and it can redirect your dog when it's distracted.

Start with your dog in a sitting position and place a treat between your fingers. Lower your flat palm to their nose level with small distance, and say "Touch." Once your dog touches your palm to try to get the treat, give it a treat with the other hand.

As a next step, once your dog gets the hang of it, you can remove the treat that was between your fingers and cue the command. Reward the successful tries only.

Note:
You can use this command is an alternative way to meet new people.

Good dog/Good boy/Good girl 14

This phrase, I would not call necessary a command. It has a similar use as "yes," so it must be used only when the dog is indeed being a good dog.

Note:

As temping as it might be, do not encourage your dog when they are stressed or scared by saying "Good dog" as it will think that it's good to be scared. So don't.

15 Settle

It's nice to have you dog chilling with you in the living room, but often it might happen that your pup wants to play, sniff, bite or watch through the window. As fun as it is, dogs must know the time and place for games, and this is how the command "settle" is important.

To teach your dog, start by luring it to step on its mat, bed or crate. Reward it every time it does and say "Yes." After a few successful repetitions, ask it to lie down and reward it once its head is on the mat or their paws. Gradually increase the time before you give it a release command and reward it.

Next step would be to move a little farther from your dog whilst it's in a settle position. If it moves, reset the command.

This command takes some time to master, especially when your dog is not tired, so keep repeating and be patient.

Note:

It's easier to teach a dog to settle in the evenings or after walks, when it's tired.

16 Bed

This command is different from "settle," in a way that the dog goes to its designated place for sleep and that it is bedtime.

Start teaching your dog by throwing a treat in its bed or crate and saying "Bed" when it steps on it to eat the treat. Follow with a "Yes." After a few successful repetitions, you can stop throwing the treat, but saying "bed" and rewarding them when it goes in it.

The next step is to ask your pup to "Lay down" once it is on the bed. Praise and reward when it does it. If the bed is in a crate, you can start closing the door for a minute or two. However, if you do not use a crate, do not give your pup the release command for a minute or two, and gradually increase the time.

As a last step, you can start moving away from them further and further. If your pup attempts to get up, say "no" and repeat the previous steps.

Note:
Going to bed should never be a punishment. Going to bed is time for dogs to truly rest, and they should want to do it and feel safe to do it.

Enough 17

It is another one of these commands that you teach when your dog is doing unwanted behaviours such as barking, digging, begging, etc. This command calms your dog down and reminds them it has boundaries.

Remember to use the command in context. The verbal cue needs to be said in a firm voice but should not sound like a punishment, so it is easy and fast to get your dog's attention and redirect their focus.

You can follow up the command with "settle" or "sit", so redirect it to the behaviour you'd like them to be doing.

18 In

This command is to help you guide your dog in the direction you want them to take – get in the car, get in the house or their kennel.

To teach it, grab some treats and throw one in the direction you want your dog to go to, and say "In" when it does. After a few repetitions, you can stop throwing the treats, but gesture and say the command, then you can reward when it does it.

If your dog is anxious to stay in the car or crate, you can leave treats and pet it there where you've asked it to go "in."

Note:
You should not reward your dog if it leaves the desired location without your release command.

Outside 19

Outside is relatively easy to teach. Every time you take your dog out for its bathroom break, say the word "outside" and over time, it will associate that word with toilet break.

Leave it 20

As dogs like to pull or chew, this command will allow you to stop them before your pup misbehaved.

To prepare for the training session, have your pup on a leash, get two different treats if your dog is food motivated. However, if your dog is toys motivated, get two different toys.

Hold a treat in front of your dog and drop the other one by saying "leave it." Your dog will try to eat it, so then say "No, leave it" and wait for your pup to look at you. When it does, say "Yes" and give right away a treat. If it pulls and gets out of position, redirect it with the leash and get your pup in the original position.

Note:

Do not let your dog eat the treat it is supposed to "leave." It's best to stop your furry friend by getting the treat or pulling him on the lead. It's important to set your pup up for success, and it to understand that good things happen when it "leaves it."

21 Bring it / Get it / Fetch

Although this is not an essential command for obedience training, it's a fun one. We all love to play fetch with our dogs.

It's pretty simple. When you throw a toy or a ball, say "Fetch" and give them a treat when they come back to you with it.

Dogs are possessive of their toys, so don't be surprised if your fur pal doesn't want to let go of the toy, so you can throw it again.

The benefits of this command are that over time, you can teach your dog to bring a specific item, not just a toy – like your remote or water bottle.

Note:

Not all dogs like to "work" or chase things. Some are lazier and won't respond to this command, so don't be surprised if that happens with your pup. It depends mostly on the breed.

22 Dinner. "Are you hungry?"

I suppose one wouldn't call this a command, as most dogs are always hungry. That said, most dogs like to know what is about to happen. Always before it's breakfast or dinnertime, I would say to my dog, "Are you hungry?" and his answer is always "Yes," or at least his tail wags in full range.

The only way for them to learn this is to always say these words before you give them their meal. There isn't other way, really.

Go for a walk. 23

Similarly, your new friend would appreciate knowing the difference between when it goes "outside" to relieve himself, or when it's the best time of the day – walkies. I can assure you, for your dog, these would be its favourite words.

Again, the only way to teach your dog is to say the words when you prep them and yourself for the walk.

Pretty soon your pup would associate you going to pick up the lead with walkies time, even without you verbally letting them know.

Note:
Your dog will get excited before every walk. Although that is fun to watch, you want it to be calm when you take it out, as there will be less pulling. Best way to do it is to not let them out before it sits or lays down calmly, even if that means waiting ten minutes before you start the walk.

24 Heel

There isn't anything more frustrating that your dog pulling you through the streets for every dog, every smell, every bird or squirrel. This is natural, but your dog must learn when it's allowed to run and explore and when it the time to walk by you.

This specific command is useful in a busy area, crossing the street or simply when you want to call your dog next to you.

Start teaching the command at home with your dog on the lead and prepare your pouch with training treats.

Call your dog's name and lure it with the treat to the "heel" position – whichever side you choose, left or right. As soon as your dog is in the position say "heel" give the treat and say "Yes." After a few repetitions, stop luring and calling your dog by its name. Just say "heel" and reward every time.

The next step is to change directions and test it to break the position. However, "heel" position should be a "stay" position as well, until you give your dog the release command.

As your dog gets better, you can start adding challenges: asking for a heel when there is a treat on the floor that he should ignore.

Take your fur pal outside and practice the command in a quiet park, before doing it in a busy area.

Note:

Don't call "Heel" until you are sure that your pup will always come into that environment. Remember, you want to always set your dog for success.

Although at first sight "heel" and "with me" command might look like they are similar, they are in fact not. They have different uses. "With me" is a cue that you use for your dog to reset and walk next to you, on or off the lead. On the other hand, "heel" is a command where your dog should come and sit next to you.

It's a really useful command in busy areas, where your dog might get distracted and would want to chase after something.

This command takes a while for you dog to truly master, so you should practise it on every walk from the very beginning. To teach it, lure your dog with a treat into a "heel" position and start walking with a treat next to its nose. You want your pooch to be looking at you.

At first, keep giving treats and saying "With me" in about every three steps and praise your dog for staying with you. Your voice should be happy and blend the words to sound like one. Yes, at the beginning you will use a lot of treats, however over time you can extend the duration between the treats.

You want to reach the point where when you call your dog on "with you," it does not move away until you give them a release command.

Note:
Do not praise your dog if it leaves you immediately after receiving the treat. It has to walk next to you.

26 This way

This command is a great way to point your dog to change their direction on or off lead when it's distracted. When you use this cue, your dog doesn't have to be walking next to you. However, it needs to follow the change of direction you have given.

At the beginning, walk with your dog on your lead and change your direction rapidly and say "This way" and lure with a treat, if it follows with no pulling, reward a treat.

After it gets the hang of it, you will not have to lure it with a treat, but keep rewarding, as it's a really important command that you want your dog to always listen to.

It's a great cue to use when you want to get your dog's attention around other dogs. Once your dog follows your direction, you can start playing and praising it, so that it chooses to stay with you.

Note:
Remember that this command must involve something exciting for your dog, whether it be a treat, praise or game.

Watch 27

It's one of my favourite commands I use to redirect the focus of my dog back on me and reset him if he gets hyper. It's relatively easy to teach, but it's important to teach it first at home where there are no distractions, and little by little use it in more challenging environments.

Start from a "sit" position and bring a treat in a diagonal position from its eyes to your eyes. Keep the repetition of the command between "watch" and "watching" whilst holding the treat and keep your voice happy. Reward when it holds the command and repeat. Train this command several times a day – before a walk, during a walk, and during playtime.

When your dog masters the first step, you can remove the treat and reward when you are ready to release from the command.

Note:
Don't use this command with an angry or stressed voice, as you want your dog to be happy to hold eye contact with you.

Paw 28

Another command from the fun zone.

Best way to start the command is to have your pup in a "sit" position. Tap the back of your dog's front foot a few times. When your dog lifts its paw, grab it and say "paw," give it a treat and say "yes." It might take a few repetitions until your pet figures it out.

Next step is to stop tapping your pup's front leg but to extend your hand and say "paw". If your dog does not get it, return to the previous step. However, with success, do not forget to reward.

Note:

At the beginning, until it masters the command, stick to the same leg and paw. Once that is mastered, teach the other paw. Start from the beginning, but change the word to "other paw", so your pup knows the difference.

These are twenty-eight handy commands that you should focus on the first year of teaching your dog. Of course, there are more commands. Of course, you can have fun and teach them more, but most of these are the core for any "good boy" or "good girl."

When do I remove the training treats?

Do not remove the treats too early. In the first, I would not recommend removing them the first year at all. Even if you think they have mastered the command, it's easy for them to revert and make a bad choice.

The more they choose not to do the command, when asked, the more they would think that they can do it when they want to, and it's much harder to untrain this bad habit. So, simply don't remove the treats. After they turn one, remove occasionally, so they don't know when they get a treat and when they do not, so they will always do the command.

Do not worry, your pup will eventually learn to obey the commands without needing a treat as a reward. A simple "Yes" or "Good, boy" will do.

Make sure to train these commands daily in five- to fifteen-minute sessions, and be patient. Your dog will revert as it goes through its different stages, as discussed in chapter four, page 56.

Remember to have fun. You and your dog should love training. It's developing your relationship – better trust, better guidance, better direction – and all dogs love to look to their owner for guidance.

Can other family members train the dog?

Yes, they can, but everyone must train with the same cue words and in the same manner, or else it will confuse your pup. In fact, it will be quite useful for everyone to take their turn at training, so your dog understands the commands that need to be followed by everyone, not only one person. Be sure that only one person at a time trains the dog, else your dog will get confused and stressed.

Learning is a never-ending journey

for YOU and

your DOG

HOW TO
STOP YOUR DOG FROM
Pulling?

Pulling is single-handedly the most common concern dog owners have, especially if the dog is of a bigger breed and can pull its owner until their face meets the ground.

It is essential to understanding why your dog pulls. It's simple. Your pup does not do it on purpose or realise that it's doing it. It is excited, and it does not possess the same impulse control as we do, so you have to teach them. We will explore impulse control on page 185, so let's focus now on just pulling.

1. Start from the beginning.

It is undeniably cute when your little pup runs excited on the lead towards something new, but it won't be so adorable when that pup turns into a full-grown dog and starts pulling you as hard as it can. So the first step into loose leash walking is to lay down the rules from the beginning and to be consistent.

Make leash walking fun with games and treats

2. Begin leash training at home.

Introduce the rule in a safe environment – what is the agreeable distance, what are the cues your dog has to pick up from you, and award the behaviour you want your pup to have outdoors. And reward the pup with treat or praise.

3.  Leave the house only when your pup is calm.

Pretty quickly your dog will know the routine before a walk, which means it will become hyper right before the walk. Do not leave the house, delay the walk until your dog is in a calm state. For example, ask your pup to sit or lay down by the door. A calm dog makes better choices.

Be consistent

Start with less busy environments

Your pup needs to understand that by pulling you, it will not get closer or quicker to its desired destination. There should be no exception to the rule. The more you walk when your dog pulls, the more frustrated it will become and the more likely it will pull.

4. Stop when your pup pulls.

Simply stopping is not enough. Your dog must remember that it's walking with you. Wait for your dog to return to you and look at you. Reward it with a treat and "Yes" and resume the walk.

You can redirect it using the "With me" command

Resume the walk once your pup returns to neutral position.

5.

6. Be patient.

As your dog goes through different stages, it will test the rules you introduced. First, it will be very excited and push you, then it will learn not to do that and so on. Never ignore this testing, always enforce the rules and give your dog time to internalise them.

LEAD WALKING
STARTS FROM Home

Being on the lead doesn't always mean a walk

Have you noticed how hyper your dog gets once it realises it's going for a walk? Have you noticed that the more hyper your dog is, the more it pulls you? It is because you have started the walk all wrong. You need to create a routine that will help you walk your dog calmly and train it to walk correctly. It will also help you teach your dog manners.

1 Create other associations with putting on the lead, besides walks.

If your dog thinks it will go for a walk when you take the lead out every time, of course, it will go crazy. Engage your dog in the lead with playing, petting, brushing, feeding and other fun things. This will create an association that taking the lead out will not mean one thing to them.

2 Put on the lead only when your dog is sitting calmly.

Do not, under any circumstances, let your dog lead you before the walk has even started. If your dog does not sit still when you are putting on the lead, stop doing it. Delay the walk. Do not chase after your dog if it's gone hyper. Say "Sit" once, and if your pup moves, leave the lead with obvious disappointment and walk away for a minute or two. Repeat until your dog realises what you are asking it to do.

3   Your dog should follow you calmly to the door.

If your dog leads and pulling before it has left the house, how can you expect it to not do it on the actual walk? Your dog manners are first taught at home, just like children. For every time your dog pulls you towards the door, you reset and delay going out.

4   Insist on door manners.

Similar as to walking to the door, your pup should wait for a release command to pass through the door. If you open the door and your dog charges off, close the door before it leaves. You want your dog to sit calmly, then you can leave, and finally, call your dog to you. Reward with praise and a treat the good behaviour, reset if your dog rushes off. Door manners are not only important for keeping your dog calm, teaching it respect, and setting the rules from the beginning of the walk, but they can be lifesaving. If your dog has the habit of running the moment the door is opened, it might run into a passing car.

5   Your dog should follow you calmly to the door.

If you put your shoes, coat, bag and the lead every time in the same order and in the same location, your dog will learn pretty quickly when it will be time for a walk, which will lead to excitement. An excited pup is an uncontrollable dog. Having this in mind, change the order of how you prepare for the walk, change the location of the lead, change where you put the lead and how long you take to get ready, all this teaches your dog patience, which is very important in training.

HOW TO
TRAIN A RELIABLE
Recall?

One of the proudest moments you will have as a dog owner is to stop your dog mid-run when they are chasing something like a bird or a squirrel.

Just imagine it.

I know, you may think it's impossible, but it is possible. However, you have to put months and months of persistent training, patience, and praise. You will achieve it.

What is a reliable recall?

Even the best-trained dogs will make mistakes. They are not robots. At the end of the day, it goes against their natural instincts – to chase, to sniff and to chase again!

Reliable recall means that your dog will make the choice to come to you when called in various situations consistently.

Why is it so hard to train?

The most important command you dog should learn.

Safe ways to train your dog recall:

- In your garden
- In a fenced off park
- With a long leash
- In a quiet field

Your pup will find it more rewarding to run after a dog or a smell than to walk next to you. Having this in mind, you know that what you offer has to have a higher value than anything they want to chase after.

You always have to be exciting and fun. Walking your dog with your nose on your phone will not help your cause. The dog will choose the bird and disobey you. If you scorn them with a negative tone or punish them, they will have more reason to do so, as they won't want to be next to an angry owner when they can continue running.

THE COMMAND

When you chose the command for the recall, we should only use it for that. Do not use it when you are calling them for attention. Be consistent. Always reward and praise, as you do not want your dog to wander if they did something right or wrong. The recall command should always be associated with positive and exciting things.

Note: If the command becomes tainted and unreliable, switch the word and start all over again.

Praise   Awards   Treads   Excitement   Walks with you must be interesting

Variety

BE FUN

Praise   Treats   Games

Games

Chase Once you call your dog to come, start running so it has to catch you. Praise and reward once it gets you.

Hide and Seek Hide behind a sofa, tree or table, and call your dog. Once it finds you, praise and treat.

Hot Potato It's a two plus person game. In turns, call your dog with the recall cue and give praise and treats when they come to the right person.

Tire your pup out at home

Puppies and some grown dogs (working breeds) can be quite restless and look forward to their walk as they a bored at home. The more bored they are at home, the more excited they will be on their walk.

During the day:
- Find time to play
- Train them
- Give them enrichment activities

If your dog thinks you are boring at home, it will be harder to make it believe you won't be boring during the walk.

TIPS

Change the treats

In my treat pouch, I have different treats mixed up together, and this way neither my dog or I know what treat it will get next.

Change the toys

As a human child gets bored with its toys, dogs get bored too. If you want them to be excited about a toy, change them up. It doesn't have to be a new toy, just a toy you have hidden away and your dog has forgotten about.

Give your dog freedom

Remember that the walk is also time for your doggy to run free. Allow time for that. After you had called them to come to you, give them the release command and give them time to sniff, run and sniff again. Of course, for their safety, either do it in and fenced off area or on a long lead.

Reward the small wins

During a walk when your pup can choose to look and sniff anywhere it likes to, but it has looked at you or come next to you – reward it. Every time. You want your dog to know that it's a good thing they checked on you. It might seem like excessive to reward eye contact, but it's an important lesson – being near you means good things.

DOs

Every walk is a training session

If you don't use every opportunity and situation, how is your dog supposed to know that it has to come to you in whatever moment you call it? Every walk, do at least a few repetitions, lead or off lead.

Walk your dog more than once a day

If you walk your dog once a day, the chance is your dog will misbehave more often than not, as it will view this walk as the only chance to have fun.

Leash your dog when uncertain

To avoid embarrassing or risky situations is best to leash your dog. Check your surroundings, observe and expect what might get your dog to run off.

Train in different situations

Your dog will learn to come to you in different situations, only if you train it in such. Start from home, move to a fenced off park, field to a dog park – the most challenging one.

Stop training when your dog loses interest

If your dog has shown no interest in you, stop training it. Find a new way to be exciting for your pup and if that doesn't work, try again tomorrow.

Involve friends and family

Your fur friend needs to learn to come not only to you, but to your other family members and other known people. It's important for them to learn that, as if they go to doggy day care or you hire a dog walker, you would want them to be well-behaved with them too.

DON'Ts

Repeat the command

"Georgie, come! Come on, Georgie, come! Georgie, come here! Georgieee!" I have certainly been guilty of doing in this. You should not beg for your dog to come, if it doesn't come to you. Either you are not interesting or your pup hasn't heard you at all. The more you call your dog, the more you enforce for them to remember that they don't have to come when called. You can repeat up to two times and if you have not achieved success, run away from them. They will most likely follow.

Set them up for failure

If you see that your dog is already distracted and you know that its recall is not at the level to interrupt it, do not call your pooch. It will be a fail, and the word will be associated with "I come when I choose to".

WHEN AND WHERE

YOU CAN HAVE YOUR DOG

Off-Lead?

It's almost every dog owner's dream to give their pup a chance to run off lead. However, it must be in a safe and controlled environment. To avoid any unexpected consequences, you must know when and where is the right time for such a run.

How do you know when you can trust your dog?

- Does your dog lack a reliable recall?
- Is your dog aggressive towards other dogs or humans?
- Does your dog like to chase moving vehicles, bikes, runners and animals?
- Is your dog always barking for no reason?
- Does your dog get lost?
- Is your dog properly socialised?
- Has your dog been de-sexed?

Yes
To Off-Leash

When you can answer NO to these questions, it's a sign that you can trust your dog.

No
To Off-Leash

If you answer YES to one or more of these, it means your dog needs to be trained more. Maybe you can let it off the lead only in fenced off and quiet areas.

Why you should be cautious about where to let your dog off the lead?

- Dangerous dogs may attack your dog.
- Your dog might attack another dog a person if it gets scared.
- It can cause a potential dog fight.
- Your dog could run onto the road and get hit by a car.
- Your dog can hump another dog or the opposite.
- Your dog can get lost in a public area.
- Your dog can get stolen.

Where is it safe to let your dog off the lead?

1. Parks

If you are going to walk your dog off lead in a park, it must be a dog-friendly park. Most parks now have signs informing when and where you can let your dog off lead. Always follow the rules.

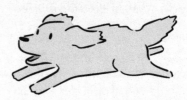

2. Private areas

There are some private properties, for example, fields and woods that off leash dogs are allowed, but you have to check if there are signs about it.

3. Beaches

Dogs are allowed off-leash at most beaches. However, in some countries, like the UK, some beaches are restricted in the summer.

4. Fenced off area

The most controlled and safest area to let your dog off lead is fenced off areas. Dogs can safely play and run around a fenced area all day long. In an ideal situation, the goodwill always be supervised by people who know what they are doing with dogs.

Where should you avoid off-lead walks?

1. Roads

Dogs should always be on the lead when crossing the road or walking on the sidewalk, especially if there's lots of traffic or pedestrians.

2. Areas that are not designated for dogs

Be wary of areas that are not designated for dogs. For example, school grounds, sporting venues, public places such as shopping malls.

3. Areas with dangerous animals

Although it is fun to watch your dog chase animals such as horses, cows and pigs, these animals may become trampled by your dog or worse, injured if they decide to attack or run away in fear.

4. Areas with irresponsible owners

Often in dog parks, you might find owners who do not have control over their dog. Unless you can trust that it won't run to another dog, I would recommend you do not let them off lead, as it can lead to a potential dog fight.

5. Building sites

Not a safe place as there are dangerous tools and heavy machinery, and waste that your dog might try to eat.

6. Hunting areas in hunting season

Be aware of where you let your dog off lead, as it can be trampled by hunters and their dogs.

THE KEY TO A WELL-BEHAVED DOG IS A LOT OF PATIENCE, CONSISTENCY, AND TIME DEDICATION.

COMMON MISTAKES
DURING **Walks**

If your dog does not behave on walks, sometimes it's frustrating, but it's usually your fault for failing to establish rules or making common mistakes over time that eventually hurt your relationship with your pet. Since dogs are social animals, they have been learning rules and respect from you since they were born. Don't hesitate to enforce the rules.

1. Not setting the rules from the beginning

If your dog is hyper before even leaving the house, it's likely that the walk will not go well. Start the walk with commands and wait for your dog to calm down before you leave the house. Show your pup from the beginning that they are not leading the walk and that they should follow you.

2. Not setting lead rules

Your pup must understand that when on the lead, it has to walk at our pace. It takes a long time for your dog to understand it and it's one reason why it might pull.

3. Not understanding your dog's body language

Knowing dogs' body language is essential to understanding how your dog feels and communicates to you in new situations, not just with people, but also with other dogs. Dogs want to trust you, knowing they can rely on you to protect them if necessary.

4. Taking your pup on the same route every

During the pup's first few months, it is not a problem. However, by the time it reaches adulthood, you will notice a pattern which might cause harm to your pet. There is a possibility that your dog will act out because of boredom or anxiety when put in unfamiliar environments.

5. Not allowing your dog to socialise with other dogs

If you never allow your dog to meet other pooches, it will remain fearful of them.

6. Too long or too short of a walk

Each breed requires exercise, but the time varies depending on their size. While some dogs can get by with thirty minutes of exercise per day, others will require at least two hours. In either case, you need to devote the time that they need. If you must shorten your walk, perhaps you could run with your dog to burn some energy. When you walk too long and over-exercise your furry friend, you may risk injury or heat exhaustion.

7. Not picking up after your dog

In most countries, it is illegal to leave your dog faeces, and you can get fined. Even if there is no one to see you, pick it up. No one likes to step on poos.

8. Being reactive

If you do not anticipate what can go wrong and don't lead your dog to make the right choices, you will be always playing the reactive game. Being proactive will save you tons of headaches.

9. Allowing your dog to go to another dog without asking the owner first

Not only can this be dangerous for your dog, since you never know if the opposite dog is friendly, but it will also cause your pup to get used to saying "hi" to every dog, and it will become highly reactive and disobedient.

10. Not interacting with your pouch

Your walk should be fun for you and your pet, not a chore. Make the most of your time together by engaging with, playing with, and training your dog. You will both benefit from it, and it will be a joyous time together.

11. Not rewarding good behaviour

You remember that if you want to encourage certain behaviour, you must reward it. How else is your dog supposed to know if what it did was correct?

12. Allowing your dog to run free with no reliable recall

It's not only for your dog's safety. It's keeping it from running in front of cars or chasing other animals.

HOW TO TEACH YOUR DOG
IMPULSE Control?

Impulse control is also known as emotional self-control. Teaching your dog impulse control can benefit you in many ways, including preventing it from jumping on you, pulling you, eating fast, stealing your food, etc. Dogs cannot magically become mature and patient by themselves. It is a skill that is learned over time.

The way a dog learns will vary greatly based on its breed or personality. Some breeds need more patience and determination than others. With these exercises and games, you will develop the skills to teach your dog impulse control.

Teach your dog to wait for a release command before their food

1. When it's feeding time, ask your dog to wait while you place the food down. Lift the bowl whenever your puppy approaches it without being released. Doing so, and waiting for a release command, teaches it impulse control. Your command is "wait" You can release your dog with the command "okay" once it has relaxed and is not jumping up to the food. To up the game, you can extend the waiting times, move far from the bowl or even leave the room. These challenges will help your dog learn to control its impulses.

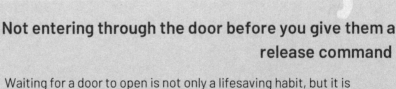

Not entering through the door before you give them a release command

Waiting for a door to open is not only a lifesaving habit, but it is also another way for them to learn to control their impulses. It's common for a dog to want to run outside for its walk, but if you keep closing the door when it tries to leave, eventually your pooch will learn to wait and the reward will come if it does. **2.**

Leave it games

Playing with your dog and throwing high-reward treats close to it while telling it to leave them. When it does, reward your pup with another treat.

3.

By leaving treats between you and your pooch and asking it to "Leave it" and "Come". Your pup must walk past the treats, ignore your them, and come to you.

Playing tug of war with your dog. Then, ask your dog to leave the toy, and disengage from the game, and then reward it with more fun.

Treats teasing games

4. Put different high-value treats close to your dog's nose but don't command it "Wait." If your dog tries to eat one without your permission, remove it. Reward your dog with the treat when it becomes bored with trying to get the treat.

If you want to up the ante, you can lay treats on your dog's paws and other parts of its body.

Reward polite behaviour

Whenever your dog gets excited and jumpy, wait until they sit and waits politely before giving them what it is they want. The equivalent of asking "please" in dog language. Once it sits, say "Yes" and reward them with whatever they waited for patiently.

5.

Note:

Impulse control is a way of teaching your dog manners and not of teaching them to how to stop unwanted behaviours such as biting, barking, etc. For that, you have to learn how to discipline the correct way and how to redirect, which we will discuss in the next pages. (187)

HOW TO DISIPLINCE YOUR DOG
THE CORRECT WAY?

A dog won't respond well to being scorned. It hurts your relationship, and the dog doesn't learn or understand what it has done wrong. The best way to discipline is to avoid accidents, poor choices and mistakes. In either case, it's your fault, as you allowed it to happen because you gave your dog too much freedom too early, ignored warning signs, or didn't train it enough.

Remember that you have a dog and not a human. Dogs have natural behaviours that you cannot prevent – *digging, chewing, sniffing.* However, to keep them from chewing and digging unwanted things, you will have to give them resources where they can safely do so.

Redirect

For example: If your furry friend steals a sock to chew, take it away and replace it with it chew toy. Do not scorn, but simply say "No" to the sock. When you replace say "Yes." In chapter nine "Enrichment Activities", page 196, we will explore games and activities that can be used for redirecting.

Interrupt the behaviour with the "No" or "Leave it" command.

If the dog is doing something it should not be doing, say "No","Stop" or ,"Leave it" right away. Do not way wait for them to make a mistake. You have to do it in a timely manner. Too late and your dog won't remember what it has done wrong.

Time-outs

Time-outs are brief, no longer than five minutes. The time-out must be clearly stated, state which behaviour you are punishing. For example, "No" for chewing, or "Leave it" for digging and time-out right away if they continue. The time-out could be you not giving them attention or you stop the game, or leaving them alone in the doggy den, but you shouldn't be putting them in their crate as a punishment. The crate should never be used as punishment.

HOW TO PREVENT
UNWANTED Behaviour?

Owners of dogs frequently fall into two categories: those who wonder what will be the next surprise from their mischievous pet when they come home and those who never have to worry about such things. Seeing as the second type is much more pleasant than the first, let's learn how to become one of them.

In order to prevent unwanted behaviours, it is best to expect them before you get a puppy. When you pup proof your house and the area where your pup will initially be (no freedom to roam the entire house), you'll notice your pup didn't create these problematic behaviours. Because there were no items left around to be chewed, you did not allow jumping up or barking, and the rules were set from the beginning. See page 41.

Prevent bad habits forming in the first place

Since the pup won't know what it is doing wrong, you can use positive reinforcement to change their behaviour in the direction you desire. For example, when it gets belly rubs, instead of biting you from excitement, give it a toy so that it bites it. If your dog needs to go to the bathroom, press the potty bell instead of barking. Reward the desired behaviour, ignore the unwanted behaviour. Dogs like to please, so they are more likely to repeat behaviours you approve of.

Focus on the behaviours you want your pup to display

If your pup has not been alone for long periods and suddenly you give them that freedom, and you find your that there has been an accident, you have only yourself to blame. The pup didn't know how to handle that freedom and what to do with itself. Increase these alone periods little by little.

Increase their freedom gradually

WHY YOU SHOULD AVOID

DOG KENNELS, HOTELS, SITTERS OR WALKERS

If You Can?

I know what you are thinking, but hear me out first. Of course, you need to know and investigate where there are such services in your area should you need them. However, it is best to avoid sending your young dog to these facilities or using these services, for the reasons listed below. If you are going on holiday, first try to contact friends and family if they can look after your pooch for the time being, and use one of these services as a last resort.

1.

They are not always experienced and/or certified .

I'm not saying that every dog owner is experienced in canine behaviour. However, if you take your dog to a professional and they do not know your dog as you do, there are risks they might not pick up on your dog's body language when it feels insecure in a specific situation.

2.

Your pup will be mixed with other dogs.

As earlier discussed, mixing different dogs together when it has not been observed before how they interact can lead to dangerous situations. In the worst-case scenario, your dog can get hurt. In the best, your dog can pick up bad habits.

3.

There is no structure.

In most of these situations, you find that your dog will be looked after for its basic needs – food, water, attention and walking. However, the structure in which dogs thrive will be missing. What does this mean? It means that a lot of the effort you have put into your training might go out the window because when they walk your dog, they most likely won't follow the rules you have created, and your dog will have full freedom to run after other dogs and/ or pull. You can expect your dog to come back naughtier with a bunch of new bad habits that it has picked up from the other dogs, and it might take weeks before you can get your dog back to where it was before.

4.

Risk of catching diseases.

Where there is a big mix of dogs and other animals, you will find a breeding ground for bacteria. Yes, to take your dog there, you prove it has been vaccinated and had had all its regular treatments, but regardless there are other diseases that one can get like kennel cough or more.

It is best if you can avoid using these services altogether. However, if you must, try to find a place with certified staff, request to see what are the conditions the dogs are kept in, and if possible, ask for your dog not to be mixed with the others and to be walked separately and always ask for pictures, videos and regular updates to see how your pup is setting in.

COMMON TRAINING Mistakes

When you train your dog, often you can get frustrated if they don't get it or make a mistake, but most of the time these mistakes are not because you don't have an obedient dog; it's just a bad training technique.

Not starting from day one
The most basic mistake. Immediately start training your pup by rewarding him with a toy, praise or treat. They form the best habits from day one with positive reinforcement, rather than leaving it until bad habits are formed.

Inconsistency
A common mistake. Do you want your dog to listen to you everywhere? At home? At the park? At the neighbour's house? Stop rewarding good behaviour, and then you'll know why they stopped listening to you.

Shouting
By scowling at your dog and forcing them into position, you are creating a negative response to that command.

Physical punishment
The result will be that the dog will associate something good with a negative outcome, rather than a positive one.

Impatience
Do not rush the dog. Give the dog time to learn. Too much pressure on the dog can cause it to react defensively or inappropriately because of being overstimulated.

Confusing your dog
- Using long words for commands
- More than one command at once
- Allowing behaviour sometimes, then others scolding it at other times
- Disciplining too late
- Overdoing it
- Using different words for the same command
- Teaching a new command with too many distractions

Giving a reward too early
If you do so, your dog won't associate the command with the reward, and understand when it has done it correct.

Giving a reward too late
If you wait too long, your dog will associate the reward with something else, rather than the command.

Expecting your dog to act like a human
You should allow your pup to explore typical dog behaviours such as sniffing, barking at birds, or rolling in dirt.

Not preventing mistakes
Dogs have natural urges such as digging, chewing, running. You can't train them to not do these things, so to avoid the mistakes by redirecting them with toys and games.

BEHAVIOUR
Issues

DON'T PUNISH - REDIRECT

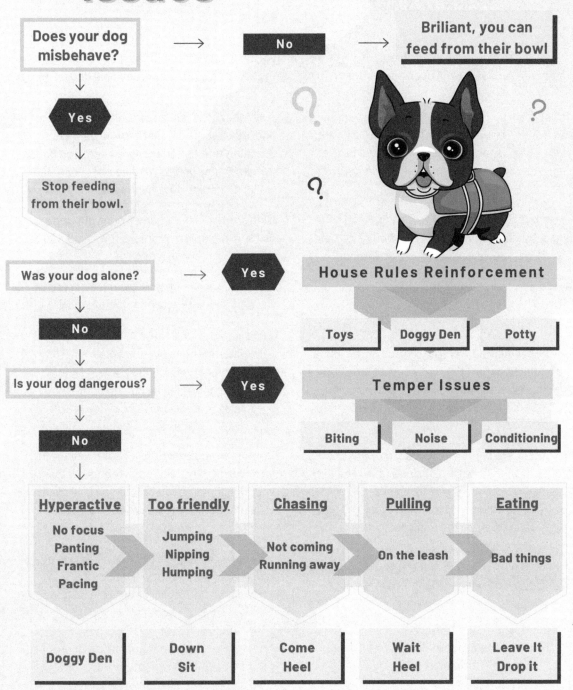

Does your dog misbehave? → **No** → **Briliant, you can feed from their bowl**

Yes

Stop feeding from their bowl.

Was your dog alone? → **Yes** → **House Rules Reinforcement**

No

Toys | Doggy Den | Potty

Is your dog dangerous? → **Yes** → **Temper Issues**

No

Biting | Noise | Conditioning

Hyperactive	Too friendly	Chasing	Pulling	Eating
No focus Panting Frantic Pacing	Jumping Nipping Humping	Not coming Running away	On the leash	Bad things
Doggy Den	Down Sit	Come Heel	Wait Heel	Leave It Drop it

THINGS TO REMEMBER
WHEN TRAINING YOUR DOG

Remember that there is no unique rule when training a dog. Every dog is different, with different temperament, and it will need adjustments. If you struggle, reach out to a professional dog trainer.

As you train your dog, you create a longstanding and trusting relationship with your pet. Our dogs look up to us for guidance, so you need to set clear rules and boundaries for them to understand.

Stay focused when you are with your pooch, and look out for any distraction, dangers or anything that can trigger your dog. You are the owner, and you have to be observant and predict what might occur.

Consistency is crucial. If you are training your dog outside, clarify that people should not pet it unless you have given them permission.

Don't repeat a command when your dog is sitting in it unless it breaks it without you giving a release.

Don't leave your dog unsupervised for a long time in the beginning.

Don't remove the treats from training too early, especially with teenage dogs.

Dogs need many different pictures of the same command before they truly understand and master it. Keep changing the locations and situations in which you train them.

Socialise – dogs can have anxiety about new experiences just like us; take them to different places and sounds, expose them to different animals and sounds, teach them social ignorance and calm behaviour in exciting places.

When they are being introduced, humans should not stuff their hands in the dog's face. The dog smell senses are powerful and can detect without putting a hand on their face. You can offer a treat, so the pup comes closer.

To improve your relationship, and make your dog associate you with good things, wait until your dog looks at you before you give them something – food, a treat, a release command, etc.

Keep the toys for interactions with you. Your furry friend needs to learn that toys have value with you.

Have low and high value treats. High value treats for when they pull for something exciting and low for any other training and for home.

Dog needs to be mentally and physically stimulated.

Don't over exercise your pup. It can cause it to become a hyperactive dog.

DOGS ARE DRAWN TO POSITIVE CONSEQUENCES, RATHER THAN NEGATIVE.

CHAPTER

TEN

DOG ENRICHMENT
Activities

WHAT ARE ENRICHMENT Activities?

Enrichment activities are a means of providing an animal with additional mental or physical stimulation. Animals in captivity rarely receive many opportunities for natural behaviours; these activities provide an essential outlet for their behaviours.

Enrichment activities can include anything that challenges the animal's mental faculties, stimulates its natural senses, or provides varied opportunities for play.

Types of Enrichment Activities

We can categorise enrichment activities into four main types: **Physical, Mental, Scent and Environmental.** These core categories explore the different natural dog behaviours, such as sniffing, digging, shredding, working for food, solving problems, interacting with other dogs, and exploring.

Most dogs will love a good balance of all the different types. However, depending on the breed, their intelligence, and their need for activity level, some dogs might prefer more of one type over the other. Providing a variety of enrichment activities allows you to explore your dog's natural interests and needs, and helps you find what really motivates it.

Enrichment activities are a great way to bond with your dog, but they also help prevent boredom, relieve stress and anxiety, provide physical and mental exercise, and socialise and train your dog.

Mix up different activities, experiment and have fun with your furry friend.

Physical Enrichment

It could vary from playing with toys to walking, to taking your dog on a run, or run next to you when you're cycling.

Mental Enrichment

These activities provide the pooch with an opportunity to solve problems, learn and experience pleasure. It could be training or food puzzles or dog agility training.

Scent Enrichment

The scent is one of the main dog scenes, which is a powerful motivator for some dogs, especially hound breeds. There are loads of things you can explore from scent games to scent training, all of which I am sure your dog will like.

Environmental Enrichment

Every time you take your dog to unknown places, you provide it with the opportunity to interact with other animals, their environments and people in natural settings.

IDEAS FOR
ENRICHMENT Activities

The following is a list of some ideas for you to use with your pets. Remember to think about the different enrichment activities and select games that will correspond with what the different category and pet finds enjoyable.

Physical Enrichment

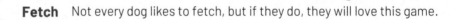

Walk   Have at least six different routes for your daily walks you can switch and keep your dog on its toes.

Chase   If you can, run and play chase with your dog.

Tug of war   Give you and your dog the opportunity to interact with you and a toy.

Fetch   Not every dog likes to fetch, but if they do, they will love this game.

Flirt pole   Similar to the fetch game, the toy is tied to a rope at one end and you can control if your dog gets it or not.

Digging pit   Create a safe digging area for your dog

Treat spot   Give your dog a treat at the same spot every day, and see if it learns to go there of its own accord, in order to wait for its treat.

Obstacle course   If you have the space, create an obstacle course with tunnels and jumps, or even got to obstacle course parks, if you have one in your area.

Training Learning and practising commands or tricks with your pup.

Mental Enrichment

Choice games Put two treats or two toys in front of your dog and let it choose which one it wants.

Agility This sits in between physical and mental enrichment, as it will provide your dog with exercise but engage its brain as well.

Food puzzles These will include Kong, lick mat, and sniffle mat. (You can buy at any pet shop.)

For recipes, go to chapter seven, page 122.

Unroll the towel Put treats in a towel, wrap it tightly and allow your dog to get the treats out.

Box search Fill a carton box with paper, more cartoons, and scatter treats. Leave your dog to work its way and find the treats.

Scent Enrichment

Scent training When you train them to recognise and search for a specific scent on a command.

Scent trails Go on a walk and have your dog pick up scents, and let them follow it. (Keep on the lead)

Scatter feeding Scatter their kibble on grass and let them sniff and search for their food.

Scavenger hunt Hide a treat, wait while your dog looks for it and reveal when they find it.

Environmental Enrichment

New locations New parks, fields, woods, beaches

New animals Take your dog to dog-friendly farms and zoos.

New people Take your dog to meet new people at parks, walks and events

New environments Pubs, shops, and other venues.

CHAPTER

ELEVEN

YOUR PUPPY
Workbook

PROPOSED PUPPY Routine

07.00 AM	Good Morning
07.10 AM	Potty
08.00 AM	Breakfast
09.00 AM	Playtime
10.00 AM	Nap
12.00 PM	Potty
12.10 PM	Lunch
12.30 PM	Playtime
02.00 PM	Nap
04.30 PM	Potty
05.00 PM	Dinner
05.30 PM	Playtime
07.00 PM	Nap
10.00 PM	Potty
10.30 PM	Good Night

YOUR PUPPY Routine

PROPOSED
ADOLESCENT Routine

07.00 AM	Good Morning
07.10 AM	Potty
07.30 AM	Breakfast
08.30 AM	Walk
09.30 AM	Playtime
10:30 PM	Nap
12.00 PM	Training
12.30 PM	Walk
02.00 PM	Nap
04.30 PM	Training
05.00 PM	Dinner
06.30 PM	Walk
08.00 PM	Good Night

YOUR ADOLESCENT Routine

YOUR
HOUSE **Rules**

On page 45, I've provided you with an example of my house rules, and the importance of them. Use these pages to create your house rules that you and your family would like to stick to.

THE DOGGY DEN AREA IS:

_____

_____

MY DOG WILL SLEEP IN:

_____

_____

MY DOG IS ALLOWED IN THE FOLLOWING PARTS OF THE HOUSE:

_____

_____

WHEN I EAT MY DOG WILL:

_____

_____

BEFORE I FEED MY DOG IT NEEDS TO:

_____

_____

THE PEOPLE WHO ARE ALLOWED TO FEED THE DOG

_____

_____

208

WHEN THINGS FALL ON THE FLOOR MY DOG:

_____

_____

IS MY DOG ALLOWED ON FURNITURE?

_____

_____

WHEN I HAVE GUESTS, MY DOG WILL:

_____

_____

MY DOG'S POTTY AREA IS:

_____

_____

MY DOG IS ALLOWED TO PASS THROUGH THE DOOR WHEN:

_____

_____

WHEN MY DOG GETS NAUGHTY I WILL:

_____

_____

BEFORE A WALK, MY DOG NEEDS TO:

_____

_____

MY OTHER PETS WILL BE AROUND MY DOG WHEN:

_____

_____

YOUR
LEAD WALKING
Strategy

As with anything in life, in order to be successful in your goal, we need to have a plan and a strategy. Use these pages to create your plan for achieving loose lead walking with your pup.

MY DOG IS ALLOWED TO SNIFF WHEN:

_____
_____
_____

MY DOG IS ALLOWED TO USE THE TOILET WHEN:

_____
_____
_____

MY DOG IS ALLOWED TO SAY HI TO OTHER DOGS WHEN:

_____
_____
_____

MY DOG IS ALLOWED TO PLAY WITH OTHER DOGS WHEN:

_____
_____
_____

WHEN MY DOG STOPS AND FOCUSES ON OTHER ANIMALS I WILL:

_____
_____

MY DOG IS ALLOWED TO HAVE FREE TIME WHEN:

_____
_____
_____

WHEN WE MEET OTHER PEOPLE, MY DOG NEEDS TO:

_____
_____
_____

IF I AM IN A RUSH, AND CAN'T FOCUS ON LEAD TRAINING:

_____
_____
_____

WHEN OTHER PEOPLE WALK MY DOG, THEY NEED TO:

_____
_____
_____

WHEN MY DOG PULLS ME, I WILL:

_____
_____
_____

I WILL LEAD TRAIN ON:

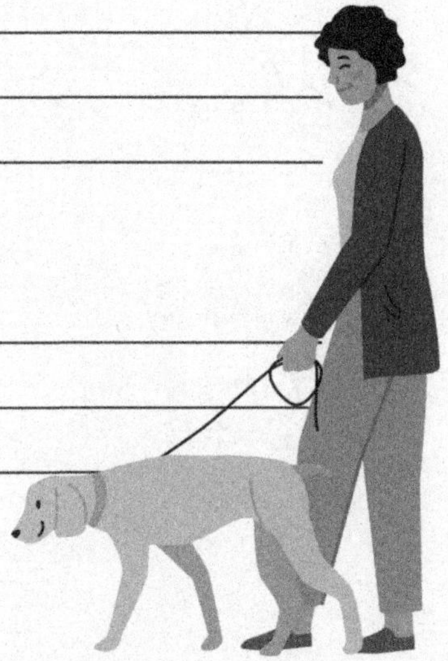

_____
_____
_____

PUPPY
DESENSITISATION Tracker

- ☑ Dogs
- ☑ Cats
- ◯ Horses
- ◯ Cows
- ◯ Sheep
- ◯ Birds
- ◯ Squirrels
- ◯ Insects

- ☑ Children
- ☑ Men
- ☑ Women
- ☑ People with accessories

- ☑ Cars
- ☑ Bicycles
- ☑ Buses
- ◯ Trains
- ☑ Groomers
- ☑ Veterinary clinics
- ☑ Pet Stores
- ◯ Pubs and restaurants
- ☑ Shops
- ◯ Construction sites
- ☑ Car parks

- ☑ Parks
- ◯ Beaches
- ◯ Rivers
- ☑ Fields
- ◯ Forests
- ◯ Lakes
- ◯ Swiming
- ☑ Different floor surfaces

- ☑ Hoover
- ☑ Hairdryer
- ☑ Cooking stove
- ☑ Washing machine
- ☑ Dishwasher
- ☑ TV
- ☑ Music
- ☑ Fireworks
- ☑ Stairs

- ☑ Sunny weather
- ☑ Cold weather
- ☑ Rain weather
- ◯ Snowy weather
- ☑ Ice
- ☑ Mud
- ☑ Puddles
- ◯ Thunderstorms
- ☑ Windy weather

Notes

PUPPY
VACCINATION
Schedule

PUPPY	CORE	NON-CORE
6-8 weeks	1. DHPP	1. Bordetella bronchiseptica
10-12 weeks	1. DHPP 2. Rabies	1. Leptospira 2. Canine influenza virus
14-16 weeks	1. DHPP 2. Rabies	1. Leptospira 2. Canine influenza virus

ADULT	CORE	NON-CORE
Annual	1. DHPP 2. Rabies	1. Leptospira 2. Bordetella bronchiseptica 3. Borrelia burgdorferi 4. Canine influenza virus 5. Crotalus atrox

PUPPY VACCINATION Tracker

WEEKS	VACCINE	DATE

ADULT	VACCINNE	DATE
Annual		

FLEA TREATMENT
Schedule

Date	Type	Dose	Notes

WORMING TREATMENT
Schedule

Date	Brand	Dose	Notes

Training

WEEK OF :

COMMAND	WEEK 8	WEEK 9	WEEK 10	WEEK 11	WEEK 12	WEEK 13	WEEK 14
	☐	☐	☐	☐	☐	☐	☐
	☐	☐	☐	☐	☐	☐	☐
	☐	☐	☐	☐	☐	☐	☐
	☐	☐	☐	☐	☐	☐	☐
	☐	☐	☐	☐	☐	☐	☐
	☐	☐	☐	☐	☐	☐	☐
	☐	☐	☐	☐	☐	☐	☐
	☐	☐	☐	☐	☐	☐	☐
	☐	☐	☐	☐	☐	☐	☐
	☐	☐	☐	☐	☐	☐	☐
	☐	☐	☐	☐	☐	☐	☐
	☐	☐	☐	☐	☐	☐	☐
	☐	☐	☐	☐	☐	☐	☐

Tracker

WEEK OF :

COMMAND	WEEK 15	WEEK 16	WEEK 17	WEEK 18	WEEK 19	WEEK 20	WEEK 21
	☐	☐	☐	☐	☐	☐	☐
	☐	☐	☐	☐	☐	☐	☐
	☐	☐	☐	☐	☐	☐	☐
	☐	☐	☐	☐	☐	☐	☐
	☐	☐	☐	☐	☐	☐	☐
	☐	☐	☐	☐	☐	☐	☐
	☐	☐	☐	☐	☐	☐	☐
	☐	☐	☐	☐	☐	☐	☐
	☐	☐	☐	☐	☐	☐	☐
	☐	☐	☐	☐	☐	☐	☐
	☐	☐	☐	☐	☐	☐	☐
	☐	☐	☐	☐	☐	☐	☐
	☐	☐	☐	☐	☐	☐	☐

Training

WEEK OF :

COMMAND	WEEK 22	WEEK 23	WEEK 24	WEEK 25	WEEK 26	WEEK 27	WEEK 28
	☐	☐	☐	☐	☐	☐	☐
	☐	☐	☐	☐	☐	☐	☐
	☐	☐	☐	☐	☐	☐	☐
	☐	☐	☐	☐	☐	☐	☐
	☐	☐	☐	☐	☐	☐	☐
	☐	☐	☐	☐	☐	☐	☐
	☐	☐	☐	☐	☐	☐	☐
	☐	☐	☐	☐	☐	☐	☐
	☐	☐	☐	☐	☐	☐	☐
	☐	☐	☐	☐	☐	☐	☐
	☐	☐	☐	☐	☐	☐	☐
	☐	☐	☐	☐	☐	☐	☐
	☐	☐	☐	☐	☐	☐	☐

Tracker

WEEK OF :

COMMAND	WEEK 29	WEEK 30	WEEK 31	WEEK 32	WEEK 33	WEEK 34	WEEK 35
	☐	☐	☐	☐	☐	☐	☐
	☐	☐	☐	☐	☐	☐	☐
	☐	☐	☐	☐	☐	☐	☐
	☐	☐	☐	☐	☐	☐	☐
	☐	☐	☐	☐	☐	☐	☐
	☐	☐	☐	☐	☐	☐	☐
	☐	☐	☐	☐	☐	☐	☐
	☐	☐	☐	☐	☐	☐	☐
	☐	☐	☐	☐	☐	☐	☐
	☐	☐	☐	☐	☐	☐	☐
	☐	☐	☐	☐	☐	☐	☐
	☐	☐	☐	☐	☐	☐	☐
	☐	☐	☐	☐	☐	☐	☐

Training

WEEK OF :

COMMAND	WEEK 36	WEEK 37	WEEK 38	WEEK 39	WEEK 40	WEEK 41	WEEK 42
	☐	☐	☐	☐	☐	☐	☐
	☐	☐	☐	☐	☐	☐	☐
	☐	☐	☐	☐	☐	☐	☐
	☐	☐	☐	☐	☐	☐	☐
	☐	☐	☐	☐	☐	☐	☐
	☐	☐	☐	☐	☐	☐	☐
	☐	☐	☐	☐	☐	☐	☐
	☐	☐	☐	☐	☐	☐	☐
	☐	☐	☐	☐	☐	☐	☐
	☐	☐	☐	☐	☐	☐	☐
	☐	☐	☐	☐	☐	☐	☐
	☐	☐	☐	☐	☐	☐	☐

Tracker

WEEK OF :

COMMAND	WEEK 43	WEEK 44	WEEK 45	WEEK 46	WEEK 47	WEEK 48	WEEK 49
	☐	☐	☐	☐	☐	☐	☐
	☐	☐	☐	☐	☐	☐	☐
	☐	☐	☐	☐	☐	☐	☐
	☐	☐	☐	☐	☐	☐	☐
	☐	☐	☐	☐	☐	☐	☐
	☐	☐	☐	☐	☐	☐	☐
	☐	☐	☐	☐	☐	☐	☐
	☐	☐	☐	☐	☐	☐	☐
	☐	☐	☐	☐	☐	☐	☐
	☐	☐	☐	☐	☐	☐	☐
	☐	☐	☐	☐	☐	☐	☐
	☐	☐	☐	☐	☐	☐	☐
	☐	☐	☐	☐	☐	☐	☐

PUPPY MEAL Planner

MONDAY

Breakfast /

Lunch /

Snack /

Dinner /

TUESDAY

Breakfast /

Lunch /

Snack /

Dinner /

WEDNESDAY

Breakfast /

Lunch /

Snack /

Dinner /

THURSDAY

Breakfast /

Lunch /

Snack /

Dinner /

FRIDAY

Breakfast /

Lunch /

Snack /

Dinner /

SATURDAY

Breakfast /

Lunch /

Snack /

Dinner /

SUNDAY

Breakfast /

Lunch /

Snack /

Dinner /

ADOLESCENCE
MEAL Planner

MONDAY

Breakfast /

Snack /

Dinner /

TUESDAY

Breakfast /

Snack /

Dinner /

WEDNESDAY

Breakfast /

Snack /

Dinner /

THURSDAY

Breakfast /

Snack /

Dinner /

FRIDAY

Breakfast /

Snack /

Dinner /

SATURDAY

Breakfast /

Snack /

Dinner /

SUNDAY

Breakfast /

Snack /

Dinner /

NOTES

_____

_____

_____

_____

_____

Expenses Tracker

DATE	DESCRIPTION	AMOUNT

Expenses Tracker

DATE	DESCRIPTION	AMOUNT

Notes

Notes

Notes

Notes

Notes

Notes

Notes

Notes

Notes

Notes

CHAPTER
TWELVE

REFLECTION
ON YOUR DOG TURNING
One

WHAT TO
EXPECT AT One Year

Depending on the size of your dog, your pup would be at a different growth stage. One-year-old dogs have typically doubled their adult size and weight. Your pup will have reached puberty too, which means you may see your furry friend humping or mounting other pups to express sexual dominance or have their first heat.

At this age, you should expect your dog to be pushing the boundaries of the rules you have created. It should be potty trained and have beginner's levels at the basic commands. Remember, you have a lifetime of your dog of constantly improving at each command.

What is next?

Puppyhood is a challenging time for both people and puppies. Now that your pup is adolescent, it's important to continue educating it with training at home and socialisation outside the home.

There will be moments when your dog will regress in its training because of hormonal changes. This is completely normal and can be expected up to the age or three, especially for bigger dogs. Do not think you are doing something wrong, or worry, just keep reinforcing the rules, repeating the commands, and eventually, your dog will get back on track.

Continue to exercise your dog daily; walks, training, and even playtime (play is still very important for a pet dog) can help keep your pet healthy at this age.

Happy Birthday!

Congratulations on your first year with your new fur friend. Take the next few pages to review what has changed with your dog, and write down your dog's progress.

8 weeks

1 year

Space For Your Puppy Paw Print

Similarities

Differences

Nicknames

MY DOG
LIKES VS DISLIKES Review

What food my dog likes

_____
_____
_____
_____
_____
_____
_____
_____
_____
_____
_____

What food my dog dislikes

_____
_____
_____
_____
_____
_____
_____
_____
_____
_____
_____

What environments my dog likes

_____
_____
_____
_____
_____
_____
_____
_____
_____
_____

What environments my dog dislikes

_____
_____
_____
_____
_____
_____
_____
_____
_____
_____

MY DOG
TRAINING **Review**

Commands my dog is good at

Commands my dog needs work on

Acknowledgements

Writing this book was a journey in itself, and I couldn't be more grateful to everyone who had a hand in it. The list of people I want to thank is endless because I would not have been able to publish it on my own.

First, I would like to thank my partner Darryl, who let me ramble day in and day out about this book and let me brainstorm and gave me ideas himself.

This Puppy Handbook would have been a much more different book if it wasn't for him. Darryl has been the most supportive partner, and I couldn't be more grateful for the trust and belief he has in me, my books and my writing. Plus, putting up with me forcing him to read it on a Saturday night, just because I panic that is full of mistakes.

To my fur baby Georgie, who I will forever think of as my little baby (no shame). For all the patience when I delayed a walk, because "I wanted to finish this page," and for all the excitement when we test another trick.

To my family, my mum, my grandma, and my great-aunt who believe in my creativity and encouraged me to pursue it, since before I could spell. I still carry your support in my heart, and I hope you cheer for me from the sky.

In no particular order to all my friends, who encouraged me and gave me feedback throughout this entire journey. Who let me ramble and show my progress, even if I was becoming the most annoying person, who gave me feedback or even helped me. Thank you: Adriana, Diego, Joe, Ilko, Denitsa, Agathe, Leslie, Andrea, Iglika.

Finally, to all the amazing trainers, for all the tips and tricks they have given me through the years. For making me a better dog owner, for the amazing work and advice which we will forever cherish in our family.

And of course, thanks to all my #booktok and #dogtok friends, you have been the most supportive and inspiring bunch.

Thank you all. I love you so much.

USEFUL DOG Organisations

Being a dog owner means you will constantly learn new things, and search for more information. Below is a list of my favourite websites I like referring to.

Fetch by WebMD
Veterinary-approved advice for dogs and their owners.

https://pets.webmd.com/

Dog Advisory Council
Focus on advice dog advice based on their breeds.

https://dogadvisorycouncil.com

BringFido
Helps you find dog-friendly places you can enjoy with your dog.

https://www.bringfido.co.uk/

Rover
Great for finding sitters, kennels or dog walkers in your area.

https://www.rover.com/uk/

OFA
Canine Health Information Centre.

https://ofa.org/

AHHA
Organisation that provides guidelines and accreditation to veterinary clinics.

https://www.aaha.org/

United Kingdom

United States

The Kennel Club
An official website for purebred dogs with tons of helpful guides and resources.
https://www.thekennelclub.org.uk/

American Kennel Club
Monitors breeding legislations and offer great educational guides and articles.
https://www.akc.org/

PFMA
Official association for pet food with helpful feeding factsheets.
https://www.pfma.org.uk/

AAFCO
Food control officials, who enforce pet food regulations.
https://www.aafco.org/

RSPCA
The largest animal welfare organisation in the UK with a great section on dogs.
https://www.rspca.org.uk/

ASPCA
An animal protection charity aiming to reduce animal cruelty in the USA.
https://www.aspca.org/

Index

Printed in Great Britain
by Amazon

35371535R00137